SBP

PSYCHOLOGY OF TEAM SPORTS

Written and compiled by
Hans Schellenberger, PhD

Edited by
Peter Klavora, PhD
Larry Leith, PhD
School of Physical
and Health Education
University of Toronto

Sport Books Publisher
Toronto

Acknowledgement To our colleagues Drs. Gretchen Kerr, Roy J. Shephard, and Adrian Taylor for reviewing this manuscript. We also extend special thanks to Dr. Susan D. Butt at the University of British Columbia for her valuable comments and suggestions. *Editors*

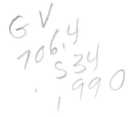

Canadian Cataloguing in Publication Data

Main entry under title:

Psychology of team sports

1st Canadian ed.
Translation of: Psychologie im Sportspiel.
Bibliography: p.
ISBN 0-920905-08-0

1. Sports - Psychological aspects. 2. Teamwork
(Sports) - Psychological aspects. I. Schellenberger,
Hans. II. Klavora, Peter. III. Leith, Larry M., 1949

GV706.4.P7913 1990 796'.01 C89-094508-X

Distribution in Canada and worldwide by
Sport Books Publisher
278 Robert Street
Toronto, Ontario M5S 2K8

Printed in the United States

Contents

PREFACE

This book is directed mainly toward those individuals interested in or needing information about the psychology of team sports. It departs from the traditional approach to studying sport psychology in several important respects. First, emphasis is placed strictly on investigating psychological parameters associated with team sports. This direction was taken due to the fact that collaborative findings dealing with methodological techniques for studying collective sport behaviour are lacking. Specific aspects of personality development in players and how they communicate and co-operate as a team have also received little scientific study to date. This book attempts to address these shortcomings by focusing exclusively on psychological factors in team sports. A second unique feature of this publication involves the description and analysis of psychological techniques specific to European researchers. Many of the psychological instruments and testing methodologies reported in this book are unfamiliar to North American coaches and researchers. As such, this project provides a cross cultural look at the field of sport psychology. Similarly, North American readers will immediately recognize that European sport psychologists tend to integrate motor learning with sport psychology in their research efforts. While this is not common practice in Canada and the United States of America, this book will illustrate several important advantages of this approach. Finally, *The Psychology of Team Sports* illustrates how sport psychology can be used as an educational methodology for developing and reinforcing collective social goals. In a manner of speaking, this approach places greater and more explicit importance on the psychological impact of sport in the socialization process.

Throughout the book, the authors have analysed meaningful psychological problems in order to improve training and education of athletes in team sports. These analyses reflect the progress made in the last several years. As a brief overview, two trends have become evident at the international level. First, cognitive components of game plays are being continually analysed. This information is then immediately put into practice, resulting in more effective game play. Second, success is seen to be due not only to the outstanding performance of individual players, but also to their co-operation and communication as a team. This finding is especially important and needs more attention in our future research efforts.

In preparing this translation, the editors have examined the material closely to avoid rash generalizations concerning the research findings. Wherever possible, specific instruments and testing methodologies are reported to facilitate replication. In a few isolated cases, however, the editors were unable to ascertain the statistical technique employed in the original research. In these instances, a summary of the research findings was presented with the caveat that the specific instrument or methodology was undetermined.

In summary, this book will provide the reader with valuable insight into the importance of sport psychology in team sports. More specifically, considerable insight into the German Democratic Republic (GDR) approach to sport psychology is revealed. The emphasis on cooperation and collective growth reflects the GDR philosophy in coaching. The reader will appreciate that this approach differs markedly from the North American perspective, where individuality is still a highly valued commodity in team sports. Although occasional references are made to a variety of team sports, soccer appears to be the major focus of research. While the book provides specific information that can be put into immediate use by the coach or sport psychologist, the editors are confident that another major value of this effort lies in its potential to generate new research ideas. The information thus gleaned will undoubtedly benefit athletic performance in team sports.

Finally, it is important to acknowledge that this book represents a continuation of GDR work in sport psychology that began with publications in 1972 and 1974. Both of these early efforts represented theoretical approaches to our discipline, and resulted in a later, more applied publication entitled *Psychology From Start to Finish*. by Dr. F. Schubert. *The Psychology of Team Sports* represents the latest attempt to look at GDR sport psychology. The publication was a joint effort by several renowned GDR sports psychologists under the direction of Dr. H. Schellenberger.

Editors

In team sports, a variety of tactical solutions and an extremely broad scope of necessary motor programmes are implemented according to the situation, the opponents' activities, and the players' tactical and motor skills.

CHAPTER 1

Psychological Aspects of Performance in Team Sports

1. Psychological Components of Performance

Performance in team sports is determined by the interaction of physical characteristics, co-ordination, technique, and tactics with psychological factors, images, operations and states; and by external conditions, such as the development in international and national standards. Cultural upbringing is just as important as physical training.

An analysis of this relationship makes it easier to understand training and competition processes. Sport psychology focuses on the psychological factors which guide and motivate player behaviour. These factors and their corresponding personality traits are revealed in socially governed and educationally oriented athletes as they cope with daily life (2:14).

Psychological components are present in four essential factors determining performance: personality, physical characteristics, technique, and tactics.

Personality

The development of personality is a continuous process. It affects an athlete's training and performance and may become decisive in competition.

Characteristics required by athletes range from general personality traits, such as a sense of responsibility, to highly specific neuromuscular and proprioceptive qualities, such as the feel for the ball. Athletes must be self-confident, responsible, persistent, independent, decisive, both impulsive and level-headed, and psychologically stable. They must be able to bear hardship, handle spectator disruptions, monitor game activity, focus and distribute attention, anticipate, observe and judge, deduce, and reason. Great demands are made on behaviour of athletes by individual risks and person-to-person combat, and by the continuous alternation of success and failure characteristic of team sports.

Since no single player has all of these characteristics, athletes must be selected to form a balanced team.

Physical Characteristics

Physical abilities (such as endurance, speed, and strength) and psychological characteristics (such as persistence, emotional stability, and concentration) influence each other and can bring athletic activity to full potential. Similarly, above-average body height can help build players' self-confidence, just as an above-average take-off power can compensate for certain disadvantages in body height. Therefore psychological components are important in the so-called purely physical factors as well.

Athletes must be self-confident, responsible, persistent, independent, decisive, both impulsive and level-headed, and psychologically stable.

Technique

The influence of psychological components becomes especially evident in the examination of co-ordination and technique. These skills are acquired by following psychological principles of learning and are governed by feelings, perceptions, images, thought, and memory processes. Success and motivation accelerate learning progress, just as a positive attitude created by doing enjoyable exercises stimulates learning. The psychological characteristics mentioned play a decisive role in stabilizing the performance of technical elements under competitive conditions.

Tactics

The finding that tactical skills can be acquired unconsciously through athletic experience, or can be taught, indicates the influence of psychological components, such as knowledge, memory, ability to switch operations rapidly, and the ability to focus and distribute attention. Despite the difficulty determining the nature of the psychological influence on player performance, the extent of this influence will be thoroughly researched, and fundamental aspects will be characterized more closely by sport psychology, in conjunction with other sciences, over the coming years.

2. Social-Psychological Aspects

Social psychology is more important in team sports than in any other type of sport. "The quality and success of a particular player's actions are determined by his own activity and by the actions of his teammates, with whom he is indirectly linked by the ball [and by tactical plans]. The degree of mutual understanding and interaction among players leads to collective achievement and game planning."(1:32)

Team interactions, co-operation, and communications are critical game factors which are indispensable for maximizing team performance. The psychological resilience and stability of a good team and its players enables team members to handle the continuous alternation between success and failure during play.

Trust between coach and athletes can be increased by including the players in every important training and competition decision. This trust encourages their sense of responsibility and their willingness to support their teammates, which in turn boosts performance.

3. Development of Selected Personality Traits

Psychological analyses of the personality traits influencing performance in soccer show that considerable differences exist between the psychological traits required in training and in competition. The need in training to drill and often carry out monotonous aspects of the game develops highly specific personality traits.

Two conclusions can be drawn. First, specific personality traits can be developed through targeted athletic education, provided that the effects of the psychological components that correspond to these training methods are recorded and defined. Second, activity-specific training methods should be given priority, since not all training methods are equally suited to the development of particular personality traits.

Soccer research, using the Pauli scale (3), shows clear position-specific differences in players (see Table 1). Some traits are more prominent in defenders than in midfield players and forwards.

Table 1 Comparison of mean personality traits for specific positions in soccer.*

Trait	All Subjects	Positions		
		Defence	Midfield	Forward
	$\bar{x}$	$\bar{x}$	$\bar{x}$	$\bar{x}$
1. Determination	2.10	2.04	2.10	2.25
2. Self-control	2.43	2.27	2.50	2.75
3. Decisiveness	2.45	2.45	2.20	2.75
4. Self-confidence	2.45	2.45	2.20	2.75
5. Long-term concentration	2.48	2.31	2.70	2.62
6. Adaptability	2.70	2.63	2.70	2.62
7. Ability to increase performance intensity	2.73	2.58	2.80	2.75
8. Impulsiveness	2.85	2.95	2.70	2.75
9. Short-term concentration	2.90	2.86	3.00	2.87
$\bar{x}$	2.56	2.45	2.54	2.71

* *Editors' Note: Sample sizes, significance levels, and the original source were not reported. Lower scores (except for impulsiveness) indicate higher levels of development in the athlete.*

The personality traits are listed according to the level of development in all players: from determination, the most highly developed trait, to short-term concentration, the least developed trait. Determination, ability to adapt, and ability to increase performance intensity are most prominent in defenders, who have the lowest level of impulsiveness. Decisiveness and self-confidence are most highly developed in midfield players.

A problem in these investigations, however, is that coaches assess players' characteristics according to training, since there they can observe and influence them over a longer period of time. Players, on the other hand, evaluate themselves according to competition. Sound criteria must be found to make an objective, accurate assessment.

Whether major differences exist (or should be allowed to exist) is a question fundamental to future investigations. Personality traits developed during training should differ as little as possible from those required in competition, since the psychological demands of competition must form the basis of the training format.

4. Implications for the Development of Psychological Components of Game Performance

The education of athletes and the development of their psychological characteristics, which become established through the relevant psychological images, operations, and states, are closely connected with their dominant activity: training and competition. Education must take place within the training process, not exclusive of or parallel to it. A fundamental basis for the development of activity-specific characteristics is a positive attitude toward training content and well-defined goals.

To realize these goals, athletes need the help and support of their coaches, teachers, and teammates. This is especially important during periods of performance stagnation and failure, when criticism can have a negative effect. Encouragement is more conducive to achievement than criticism in all situations

Psychological attributes which are necessary for performance evolve only within the framework of the activity itself. Anything that we do not require of our athletes in training and in preparatory competitions will not materialize in critical situations or competition. Training requirements should therefore resemble competition standards as much as possible. Training methods should be analysed to determine their effects on the development of psychological components, and implemented accordingly.

Finally, we wish to stress the great potential for performance improvement that comes from solid relationships. A precise analysis of collective relationships during critical stages of development forms the coaches' basis for directing the team. Friendships among players which go beyond training and competition should be developed, as well as the objective performance relationships which are directly required in game activity.

Team sports demand genuine collective relationships. Playing must be enjoyable. Playing with friends is one of the most fundamental attractions of team sports.

CHAPTER 2

Cognitive Functions in the Psychological Control of Performance and Implications for Coaching Team Sports

1. Tactical Determination of Game Manoeuvres

The quality of athletic performance is determined by many factors. From a psychological point of view it is a combination of motivational, volitive, emotional and cognitive processes expressed in motor activity specific to team sports. The player's cognitive faculties occupy a central position within the system of factors in team sports that have a determining influence on performance.

Athletes must continually come to terms with a multiple reference system: teammates, opponents, ball, goal, and room to move. Since all game plays are tactically determined, a diverse and complex set of demands is made on the athletes' abilities to receive and assimilate information. This reception and assimilation takes place under great physical and psychological stress over a relatively long period of time. Because all defensive and offensive manoeuvres in competition require decisions based on specific and rapid perception of the situation, thought and memory are integral to success. In team sports, a variety of tactical solutions and an extremely broad scope of necessary motor programmes are implemented according to the situation, the opponents' activities, and the players' tactical and motor skills. The success of tactical play in competition largely depends on the level to which athletes' perceptive and intellectual faculties are developed, especially in association with other performance-determining factors. Trends in the international level of performance and literature on this subject point to the importance of cognitive performance in achieving excellence in team sports. This suggests the need for a more subtle analysis of cognitive demands made on team players. Cognitive processes (those psychological processes which form the basis for and the cause of mental functions) are learning processes which aid in current motor orientation and motor control. An analysis of the cognitive processes is based on the premise that the dynamic and activity-specific processes which make up an activity select and emphasize these functions and their interaction at varying levels, depending on

In team sports, a variety of tactical solutions and an extremely broad scope of necessary motor programmes are implemented according to the situation, the opponents' activities, and the players' tactical and motor skills.

the goal being pursued. These processes are determined by laws governing the reception, assimilation, and storage of information.

By analysing constantly changing situations in the playing environment, and by anticipating future conditions and the results of their own actions, players are able to decide consciously what actions to take and how to affect game play within the framework of motor control. A fundamental condition for this is the human ability to apply general environmental images and operational rules to a concrete situation and to control and regulate one's own actions, keeping in mind specific goals, demands, and conditions.

The different structural units of motor control involved in game manoeuvres include control of orientation, motivation, decision-making, execution, and evaluation of feedback.

It should be emphasized that the individual psychological components of motor control operate not sequentially, but simultaneously, as a unit. Depending both on objective and subjective conditions at different stages of activity, however, specific functions may become more prominent (11).

2. Demands Made on Cognitive Functions During Orientation Control of Game Manoeuvres

Orientation control, or motor orientation as a "guiding mechanism of the activity process" (2), includes all the processes which aid in the acquisition of "external" information (predominantly graphic and linguistic-conceptual) and in the acquisition of the reproduction of "internal" information (stored in memory) needed for the development of an activity programme. Sensory information reception and storage, as well as acquired motor experience, form the basis of orientation control. They are the prerequisites for the players' "inner model" (operative image system) of the game situation, which can have various subjective levels of abstraction, differentiation, and awareness. The extent and nature of the reproduction and assimilation of these prerequisites have a decisive influence on the result of the action. Motor orientation is critically important to the overall progress and is the result of technique and tactics, and it is the basis and continual reference point for other mental processes during all stages of motor control. Among the aspects of motor orientation we find integrated systems of mental images, processes, states, and characteristics. The function of these systems is to analyse external conditions, relevant motor experiences, and possibilities for specific activity goals; to elaborate concrete measures to realize these goals and to establish a plan of action; and to develop a framework to monitor the execution of these actions (10:19).

In order to be in a position to orient their actions on the playing field, players must be able to perceive in diverse ways the situation around them and its relationship to their own activity (Diagram 1).

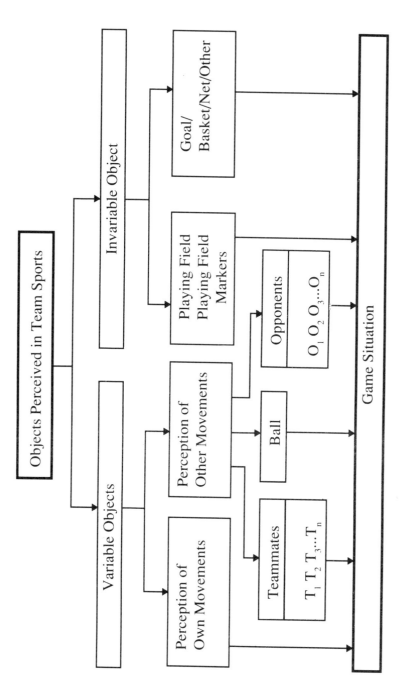

Diagram 1   Classification of objects perceived in team sports.

Analyses of play and an assessment of all relevant literature suggest that several specific demands are made on players' spatial and motor perception. These demands are shown in Diagram 2.

Spatial perception reflects the spatial relationships between various objects in the players' environment. Motor perception reflects changes in position over a period of time and includes temporal perception, which reflects the duration, speed, and sequence of events. Players must be able to perceive with subtlety not only their own movements, but also anticipate the movements of teammates, of opponents, and of the ball.

Spatial and motor perception are determined by several factors:

1. A broad visual field results from the large number of objects (opponents, teammates, ball, goal) that must be perceived within a relatively large area, i.e., playing field and it requires good peripheral vision.

2. Because of constantly changing game situations and a great diversity of possible player movement, new stimuli are continually present and must be assimilated. Players must focus on what is most important in what they perceive. This is known as selective attention. Players' own activities complicate matters further, since the manoeuvres they adopt depend on the developing game situation.

3. Complex conditions (ball velocity or spin, difficult weather conditions, or feinting by the opponent) make high demands on accuracy of perception.

4. Critical moments in the game when the player is under pressure demand immediate and high quality perception for a short period of time to ensure correct tactical decisions.

5. A high quality of perception must be maintained throughout the playing time in spite of elevated physical and psychological stress (pressure to do well, influence of opponents, spectators and referees, feelings of failure, etc.).

Players must be able to see the game situation as a complex unit; and they must be able to localize themselves within the entire system of playing field, teammates, opponents and ball. This is called "orientation capacity" and governs how players observe and control their own movements relative to changing demands.

The quality of perception depends both on the objective stimuli, such as intensity, complexity, and contrast, and on the functional levels of reception and analysis of information. It is largely influenced by concentration, motivational processes (goals, beliefs, attitudes, motives, needs, interests, ideals, etc.), volitive regulatory processes, and the players' emotional states, knowledge, and experiences (material stored in memory).

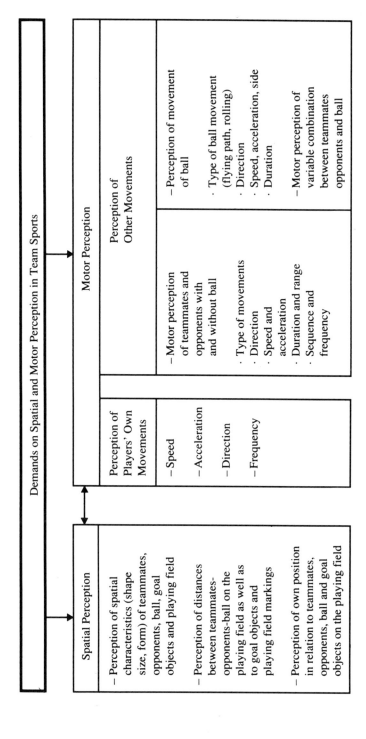

Diagram 2   A summary of the demands on visual perception in team sports.

3. Demands Made on Cognitive Functions During Motivation and Decision-Making Control of Game Manoeuvres

Motivation and decision-making lead to the production of motor activity through orientation control. This controlling complex determines the objective, content, intensity, duration, and outcome of the activity. Especially significant are valency experiences: needs, interests, attitudes, and motives. The close interaction between sensory information received and assimilated and the information already stored in the memory enables players to carry out actions appropriate to the situation.

Decision-making is the ability to make quick, accurate tactical decisions—it is one of the most important abilities of an athlete. This type of instantaneous analysis takes place during competition and differs from thought processes which occur at other times. It often determines the success of technical and tactical plays and is frequently responsible for differences in individual performance.

The quality and speed of a player's decision-making during play depend on factors such as speed and accuracy of information reception; activation level; correct use of various features of concentration; tactical knowledge, skills and experience; and motivational, emotional, and volitive factors.

Anticipation, which is closely related to mental images, is necessary for motor decisions made within the framework of tactical thought. During play, great demands are made on players to anticipate the tactical intentions of teammates and opponents and to formulate their own plans for action. In addition, players must anticipate the movements of the ball in connection with their own movements and the movements of teammates and opponents (path of the ball during the execution of their own actions, or ball being passed by teammates or opponents). These demands are shown in Diagram 3.

Additional demands on player anticipation should be mentioned:

1. Complex game situations make it impossible to anticipate individual events. Players must anticipate simultaneously the constant changes in the flow of the game, their own movements, and the movements of others and of the ball.
2. Players must make allowances for alternative actions of teammates and opponents who may be near or far away.
3. It can be difficult to anticipate when there is frequent feinting. This is often observed in games against unknown and therefore unpredictable players and teams.
4. Players must anticipate a maximum amount of action using a minimum

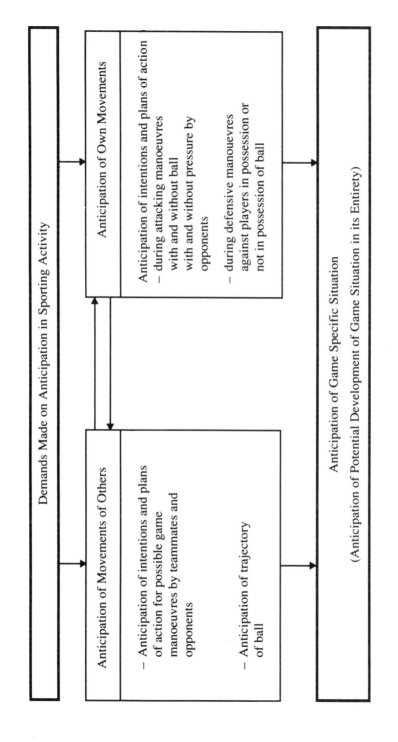

Demands Made on Anticipation in Sporting Activity

Anticipation of Own Movements

Anticipation of intentions and plans of action

– during attacking manoeuvres with and without ball with and without pressure by opponents

– during defensive manoeuvres against players in possession or not in possession of ball

Anticipation of Movements of Others

– Anticipation of intentions and plans of action for possible game manoeuvres by teammates and opponents

– Anticipation of trajectory of ball

Anticipation of Game Specific Situation

(Anticipation of Potential Development of Game Situation in its Entirety)

Diagram 3   A summary of the demands made on anticipation in team sports.

amount of information under pressure of time.

5. Players must use long-term anticipation. Anticipation cannot be restricted only to those actions which will occur next; it must encompass complex sequences of movement and tactics that may occur throughout the course of play.

6. A high quality of anticipation must be maintained for the entire playing time, notwithstanding elevated physical and psychological stress.

Players are therefore faced, generally, with a very large number of alternatives in deciding on a specific action (16). Making an appropriate decision while under pressure in competition depends on the situation at hand, overlapping goals, and behavioural norms. This is a highly intricate psychological process. Players must bring their objectives into line with the prevailing conditions, and these conditions must be related to previous and subsequent possibilities for performance and behaviour.

Decisions are determined by objective and subjective factors. The game situation constitutes the objective basis for making a decision. Subjective factors such as general motivation, intensity of will, intellectual development, technical knowledge, tactical knowledge, and experience must also be considered.

In analyzing the literature, it is necessary to qualify more closely the various demands which are made on players' decision-making behaviour.

Diagram 4 illustrates the stages of the decision-making process in sports. Because of the number of teammates and opponents and the wealth of options available, players are faced with complicated decision-making conditions. In order to make the best decision players must first quickly consider several possible variables. Then they must consider the objectives of their action (e.g., a shot on goal) and devise a suitable plan of action (e.g., the execution of a specific variation of a wide jump shot in basketball). The final step involves trying to implement that action.

Work in motor analysis has identified additional demands on decision-making in team sports:

1. The conditions and situation for making decisions are constantly changing.

2. Based on their mastery of tactics and technique, players must decide on the action best suited to their purposes, and they must do so within the limits imposed by the rules of competition.

3. There is an irregular alternation between "sure" decisions made in clear-cut situations, risky decisions made in ambiguous situations where the probability of success is small and the outcome is questionable, and "uncertain" decisions

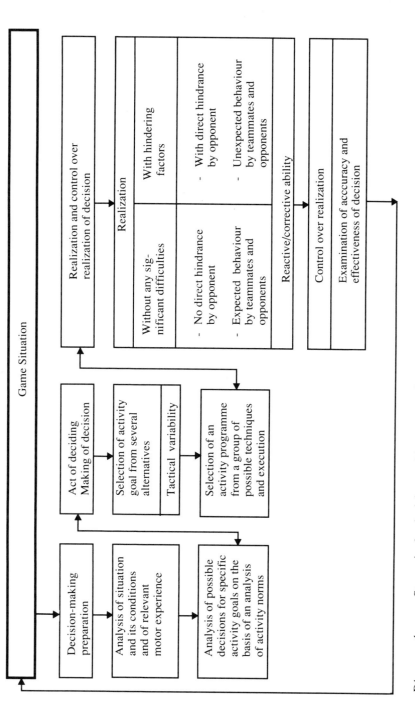

Diagram 4   Stages in the decision-making process for technical and tactical game manoeuvres.

made hastily in very confused situations where the outcome is unknown.

4. In order to be successful, players must be capable of making quite different decisions in similar situations; opponents tend to adapt quickly to decision-making which results in uniform and predictable behaviour.

5. Often players are compelled to make decisions which have permanent effects on the game. Such decisions influence sequences of events as well as the immediate situation.

6. The execution of collective tactics requires collective decision-making. Decisions concerning game plays to be carried out by two or more players must be precisely coordinated according to spacial and temporal sequences. Examples include free-kick combinations, zone defence, and blocking.

7. Many decisions must be made under extreme time constraints. The time available to make the best decision regarding tactical goals and technical methods is extremely limited. Hesitation, indecision, helplessness, or inhibition—all of these prolong the time required to make a decision. Even hastiness, as well as taking too much time, can cause incorrect decisions.

8. Decisions about actions to follow must be made during the execution and monitoring of actions already decided on. Players must think while under the influence of heightened emotions brought on by spectators or opponents. Certain emotions, such as the feeling of success, may serve to increase the intensity and precision of the thought processes, while others, such as the feeling of failure or lack of self-confidence, may have an inhibitory effect.

9. A high quality of decision-making must be maintained throughout the game despite elevated physical and psychological stress.

4. Demands Made on Cognitive Functions During Execution and Evaluation of Feedback of Game Manoeuvres

Execution and evaluation of feedback include the psychological factors which, after decisions are made and plans of action established, ensure the execution, feedback, and evaluation of an action. This directs relevant motor sequences, including reafferent continuous control (motor-guided and regulative reafferents). Orientation control is a constant point of reference. Execution control occurs at various or graduated levels (3). The differences between sensory-motor, perceptual-conceptual, and intellectual-regulatory levels affect the scope of cognitive conveyance, its sphere of influence and consciousness. Which regulatory

Players are faced with a series of complex conditions while executing an action because of opponent interference.

level will be dominant during a certain athletic activity depends on the specific demands made by the activity and on the player's fitness level.

Motor execution of a game manoeuver is the visible result of all previous and ongoing psychological and physiological processes. Criteria for evaluating performance exist. The following demands on the execution of a motor action in sports should be emphasized:

1.   Fostering motor skills in team sports requires the use of an extremely wide variety of motor programmes, with and without the ball.
2.   The ability to vary the execution of an action appropriate to a situation is required. Variability is needed to ensure teammate co-operation, and to deal with opponents, objects, and environmental influences.
3.   An action can be executed at various speeds according to tactical needs.

This requires good motor co-ordination, especially in connection with the ball.

4. Great demands are made on precision during the execution of activity programmes in terms of goals and sequences. In team sports the accurate accomplishment of the final objective is much more important than the exact completion of a motion according to sequence. To move precisely at high speed is nevertheless essential.

5. Players are faced with a series of complex conditions while executing an action because of opponent interference. In rebound plays, players select and set up defensive plays in order to create difficult conditions, and to force opponents to make mistakes. Direct opponent interference is even more complicated.

6. Players must achieve and maintain a high level of effectiveness in executing their actions throughout the game while coping with elevated psychological and physical stress.

In conclusion, it should be stressed that perception and deciding on subsequent action take place during actual motor execution, closing the circle of cognitive demands made on the player (12:814).

5. Cognitive Functions in the Technical and Tactical Training in Team Sports

Cognitive functions in players can only be trained and developed within the process of coming to terms with their environment. Psychological processes always control activity, and therefore skill development is considered a dependent part of general personality development. The level to which a skill can be developed depends upon the state of overall personality development.

In the specific development of cognitive functions there are still appreciable reserves for the continued growth of performance in team sports. The development of the cognitive functions necessary for excellence in sports must not be allowed to take its own natural course; it must be controlled sensibly and methodically. The quality of mental processes such as perception, anticipation, decision-making, and information reception and assimilation can be improved through goal-oriented training using several steps integrating these functions with motor activity. Players must carry out these functions as quickly as possible and maintain proper techniques throughout the game while under psychological and physical stress.

The methods used for the technical and tactical training of players must be selected in accordance with general goals and objectives, and then implemented, focusing on a specific goal. The development, stabilization, and perfection of players' technique and tactical performance require an effective and methodical training structure modelled as follows:

Stage 1: Acquisition, stabilization, and perfection of technical skills.

Objective: To acquire and consolidate individual and collective motor techniques and movement combinations without tactical objectives; and to coordinate the movements of individual players temporally and spatially with those of their teammates.

Method: Training and competitive forms of preparation with standardized or variable conditions without active opponents (set motor sequence).

Stage 2: Development, stabilization, and perfection of situation-governed technical and tactical skills, and actions.

Objective: To develop observation, anticipation, and decision-making for the completion of tactical objectives and to stabilize the execution of appropriate motor activities under non-competition conditions.

Method: Training methods range from hypothetical situations with relatively few alternatives to complex game forms with conditions similar to those in competition.

Stage 3: Development, stabilization, and perfection of complex game skills.

Objective: To develop and use individual and collective technical and tactical manouevres for a mastery of offensive and defensive plays in competition; to develop rapid and accurate information reception and storage.

Method: Exercise and training games with specific goals: Conditions which exceed competitive demands are created, including the overload method, which uses rings, higher nets, smaller goals, etc. This stage is important since the previous stages do not overtax players' cognitive abilities or meet the diverse, complex demands made in competition. Training should consist of games using full, reduced, or unequal sides to increase difficulty. Structured games against unknown teams of equal strength should be scheduled. Other team sports should also be played to develop cognitive functions.

Stage 4: Use of complex game-playing ability in competition.

Objective: To attain optimum technical and tactical performance for each player and for the entire team under maximum physical and

	psychological stress.
Method:	Competitions.

The objective and measure of all efforts is competition. It places the greatest demands on the players' diverse abilities and skills, both individually and collectively; and it aids in the continual perfection of playing fitness, which cannot be replaced by any other training.

These stages should be variously emphasized in training to develop the competitive condition of the players. They will make complex demands on perceptive, intellectual, and motor processes (8:12). A fundamental principle of training is the reciprocal process of establishing requirements and implementing them during competition, a process from which new requirements arise.

Players should learn the importance of training methods in developing cognitive functions specific to team sports. For the development of these functions, players are to be instructed in the important use of training methods such that the intended results are actually achieved:

1. Development and perfection of situation perception through the training of:
   • spatial and motor perception (teammates, opponents, ball) in immediate vicinity and farther off;
   • visual perception range (number of objects to be perceived), perception accuracy and perception speed;
   • rapid alternation in perception orientation (ball, goal, opponents, teammates);
   • rapid apprehension of main objects of focus.
2. Development and perfection of situation anticipation through training of:
   • anticipation of course of action of teammates and opponents, including possible alternatives for action and deceptive manoeuvres;
   • anticipation of trajectory of ball, especially under more demanding conditions (high speed of ball, side, wind, several balls);
   • successive and simultaneous anticipation of sequences during individual and team tactical attacking/defensive manoeuvres under pressure.
3. Development and perfection of decision-making behaviour through training of:
   • decisions regarding goals of actions and courses of action with the objective of optimum decision-making given an increasing number of alternatives for actions;
   • invididual and team decisions and sequences of decisions under pressure for the realization of individual and team tactical offensive and defensive

Players should learn the importance of training methods in developing cognitive functions specific to team sports. For the development of these functions, players are to be instructed in the important use of training methods such that the intended results are actually achieved.

manoeuvres;

• the ability to resolve in an optimum manner decision-making conditions which are particularly more demanding (continual chage in situation; inclusion of additional teammates and opponents during the execution of game manoeuvres at high speed, etc.).

4. Development and perfection of motor execution through the following:

• situation-specific training programmes based on the making of correct decisions concerning goals of actions by means of a continual change of situations, numerous movement combinations, and intensive influence from opponents;

• high manoeuvre speed in connection with great demands on accurancy of manouevres (shooting/passing accuracy);

• manoeuvres performed under increased physical and phychological stress.

In summary, the complex technical and tactical processes and methods used in training place extremely great demands on coaches, physical education teachers, and players. To realize effective progress in performance and to optimize the necessary processes of information reception and assimilation, a high degree of conscious and intensive player cooperation is required.

CHAPTER 3

Concentration and its Relevance to Team Sports Players

1. Concentration in Athletic Activity

An investigation into the psychological elements of athletic performance cannot overlook the question of concentration in sports: concentration is indispensable to performance in training and competition. It has become, at the same time, the subject matter of a number of widely divergent psychological viewpoints. Perhaps no other psychological phenomenon is more disputed. Some psychologists entirely discount the role of concentration in sports while others give it virtual parity with other psychological functions. After examining the concepts held until the present time (5) a few of the basic approaches to concentration in sports are presented before taking an in-depth look at the importance and diagnosis of distributive and focusing functions of concentration.

The basic shortcoming of all previous attempts to examine and explain concentration lies in the fundamental scientific principles which isolate each individual function and do not examine these functions as an expression of the entire personality. We attempt to examine this problem on the basis of Marxist-Leninist psychology and its dialectical and material conception. The premise of this viewpoint is the close relationship between consciousness and activity, man and his world, subject and object, ideal and material, and which recognizes the psychological elements as being a feature of higher nervous activity. According to the Soviet views on personality, concentration is a psychological variable which entails an examination of man as a complex, diverse, dynamic, and functional biosocial unit in view of his behaviour, achievements, and developmental history. Concentration should not be defined solely by reference to its mechanisms, as functional psychology still does today; it should be defined also by reference to the entire personality and its dynamics.

Conflicting views on the theoretical foundations of concentration are based on "the premise that concentration is not an independent process and has no specific product" (1:15). In our view, concentration should be understood as a factor in the interaction between the organism and its environment (3:313;

15:559). This factor expresses the complex relationship between subject and object, in which the object draws the subject's attention by exerting a highly sophisticated attraction. Not only does the object appear different to each subject, it can also appear different to one subject under different conditions.

It is to no small extent because of man's capacity to concentrate that his is unique among the higher primates, that he is able to adapt in so many different ways to his environment, and that he is able to focus attention very precisely on certain aspects within it and, in this way, to radically transform it. Needs, interests, ideals and attitudes, as well as the individual's goals (i.e., his entire motivational structure), play a fundamental role.

In this light, perception and thought are not isolated from the subject, which thinks and feels, nor independent of the object, which is the focus of thought and perception. Concentration expresses this dialectical relationship between the individual and his environment, through the continual exchange and assimilation of information (3:31). Accordingly, concentration is not a psychological process as such, but a particular aspect of all psychological processes (15:554; 16:265; 2:131; 9:172).

Concentration is analysed in terms of its orientation function, its role in the conscious regulation of alertness levels (i.e., vigilance), and, more generally in terms of its role in all cognitive activity (3:503). Furthermore, according to Galperin (1:10) concentration reduces the time needed for mental activity.

Concentration is also selective in nature; of all the objects, processes, and other stimuli which surround us, only a few can be clearly perceived, consciously assimilated, and acted upon. For this reason a complex process of selection, dependent both on subject and object, must be carried out.

In addition to regulating, focusing, and selecting, concentration also causes a structural change in the psychological process. This change is called 'sensitization' (15:557; 17:161; 3:481). Sensitization appears in conjunction with experiments on vigilance in industrial and engineering psychology, in the form of dynamic activity and intensity of information assimilation (3:481; 11:31; 12:285). Sensitization is a perceptual process in which there is a transition from listening to hearing, from looking to seeing, and from observation to methodical perception. The clarity and graphic quality of perception are increased and the absolute threshold of sensation is lowered. When concentration is applied to mental processes and actions, sensitization results. Mental processes then become more intensive, generating a prerequisite for creative mental activity. Haphazard and spontaneous movements then become deliberate and planned activities (15:555; 1:15). Generally speaking, this process leads into a specific goal-oriented activity.

34

Concentration is also selective in nature; of all the objects, processes, and other stimuli which surround us, only a few can be clearly perceived, consciously assimilated, and acted upon. For this reason a complex process of selection, dependent both on subject and object, must be carried out. Without concentration athletes would be unable to perform in sports, where great demands are placed on the mastery of motor activity and on the capacity to continually adapt to training and to competitive conditions in direct and indirect confrontation with opponents.

In summary, we define concentration as a selective, regulatory and directing function of human consciousness; it is a process in which the dialectical relationship between subject and object, consciousness and activity, finds expression. Concentration is subject-related insofar as it is determined by the motives and goals of individuals. But it is also object-related, since it is determined by the concrete, specific nature of the objects acting on it. It is a particular aspect of the psychological process and is directly related to its structural change through sensitization (i.e., conversion to goal-oriented activity). This definition clearly delineates the position of concentration within an individual's psychological processes and personality traits.

From the point of view of the dialectical relationship between subject and object, there are two types of concentration: voluntary and involuntary. However, it would seem appropriate to ignore this formal distinction, because both the "elementary, vitally directed" as well as the "complex, cognitively directed" turning of attention bring, in principle, "the same central nervous activities into play" (3:503). In addition, the predominance of voluntary or involuntary concentration is merely a question of emphasis during the interaction between the organism and its environment. As such, it does not affect the process itself.

Concentration is controlled by an individual's activity; its conditions vary according to the demands made on it. Sport provides a framework for the investigation of concentration which is different from the frameworks provided by work, learning, artistic creation, play, and other human activities. Without concentration athletes would be unable to perform in sports, where great demands are placed on the mastery of motor activity and on the capacity to continually adapt to training and to competitive conditions in direct and indirect confrontation with opponents.

If we analyse the significance of concentration in sports, we can determine that the selective attention given to certain objects and actions, the regulation of the close interaction of mental and motor factors, and the sensitization of psychological processes needed to mobilize full strength for competition are criteria for concentration, as well as fundamental aspects of athletic performance. They are expressed in terms of the close interrelation between motivational characteristics and the goals of the athlete's personality and in terms of the concrete nature of objects and actions in sports in the form of goal-oriented activity.

We shall discuss the importance of concentration in sports first in very general terms. Although sports make complex and specific demands on player concentration—especially in terms of intensity, duration, scope, and capacity for switching concentration—they also promote its overall growth. In this

Sports make a concrete contribution to the optimum development of the athlete's entire personality. The high degree of synchronization of perception, tactical thinking, and motor activity becomes instinctive in nature and requires players to alternate continuously and rapidly between distributive attention and focused attention, especially during quick-paced game activity.

respect, sports make a concrete contribution to the optimum development of the athlete's entire personality.

Editors' Note: In this chapter the terms 'concentration' and 'attention' are used, for the most part, synonomously, but on some occasions with a slight distinction. Attention is defined as the process of focusing consciousness to produce greater vividness and clarity of certain objects relative to others. It involves several abilities, such as focusing, distributing, and switching.

Concentration, on the other hand, will be used more generally to denote the directing of attention towards a single object or objects.

2. Demands Made on Scope and Switching of Attention and its Significance for Performance in Team Sports

All elements of attention are required in team sports. Particular emphasis, however, should be placed on distributive attention (the ability to attend to several objects or actions at once), focused attention (the ability to limit the scope of attention to one object or action), and the ability to switch attention from one object or action to another.

The elements of attention mentioned above are derived from the multiple reference system in which the player is active. Players must bring their motor and tactical play into line with the goal, the ball, and with the relatively large number of teammates and opponents who directly or indirectly influence them within the framework of a relatively large, but also limited, playing field. Players must keep specific rules in mind while striving for maximum team success and cooperation. The sheer number and variability of these factors make it necessary for players to have a wide perception range, and this, in turn, implies that they must have well-developed distributive attention.

The high degree of synchronization of perception, tactical thinking, and motor activity becomes instinctive in nature and requires players to alternate continuously and rapidly between distributive attention and focused attention, especially during quick-paced game activity (14:49). Since it has a considerable effect on accuracy, the ability to switch attention from a broad to a narrow range, and vice versa, is especially critical during scoring attempts near the goal. We were able to establish this conclusively in several investigations (4; 7; 13). A compilation of previous results shows that without being hindered in any way, the *additional* attentional demands on opponents and teammates caused a considerable decline in the number of successful baskets and shots on goal. This result can be attributed to the fact that the range of attention expands during the

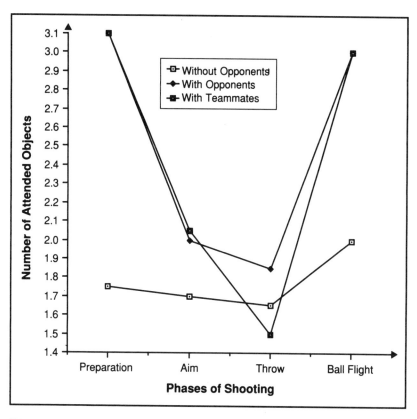

Figure 1   Distribution of attention during shooting in basketball – player not moving

shooting action, making it difficult to focus solely on the goal.

In further investigations (4; 13; 18) it was possible to prove that there was indeed an alternation between highly distributive and focused attention during shooting attempts on goal. Figures 1 to 7 clearly show the progression of changes in attention range during the separate stages of shooting actions in basketball, soccer, handball, and volleyball, whether from stationary or moving positions. These graphs show clear differences in all four activities between the simple demands made in stationary motor sequences (i.e., movements made from standing position or when ball is stationary; without opponents, teammates, and goalkeeper) and the more complex demands made where conditions most resemble competition (i.e., where goalkeepers, opponents, and teammates are a

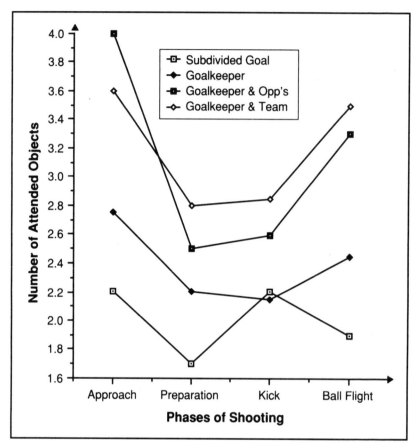

Figure 2   Distribution of attention during shooting on goal in soccer – ball stationary.

factor for consideration). Complicated situations in competitions, where at least two teammates or opponents may influence game activity, can increase the demands made on the distribution and switching of attention even more. Nevertheless, in all four team sports, players' attention focuses on objects involved in accurate movements during shooting actions from standing or moving positions. This is shown by the decrease in the number of objects and actions the player attends to during the throwing (handball), shooting (basketball, soccer), or hitting stage (volleyball).

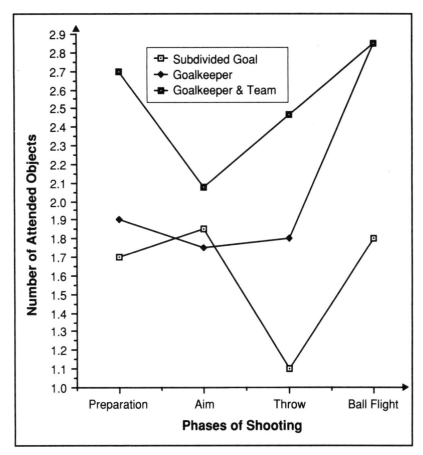

Figure 3   Distribution of attention during shooting on goal in handball –
player not moving.

In Figure 8, distributive attention in all four team sports is shown for attempted shots on goal from a moving position with an opponent present (including goalkeeper in soccer and handball). The differences between the four team sports clearly show how complex conditions differ, even within a sports category. It is interesting to note that the complex distributive attention during shots on goal in soccer and attacking shots in volleyball is evident throughout all stages of the shooting activity (with a broader concentration range). In these examples, "a double concentration" is present to a certain extent; the primary

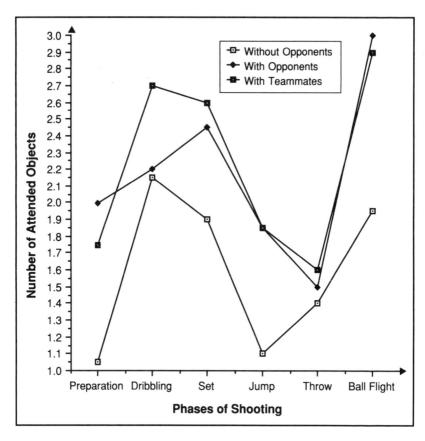

Figure 4   Distribution of attention during shooting in basketball – player in motion.

objective being the ball, the secondary objective being the free unoccupied area of the goal or playing field. This means increased demands on the scope and the switching of attention. Conclusions drawn from Table 2 show that there is a considerably greater dispersal of goal activities in both of these team sports as opposed to handball and basketball, where players must concentrate on only one goal. On the basis of the results presented in the graphs (Figures 1 to 8), it is possible to recommend the correct behaviour in team sports, both in respect to switching from distributive to focused attention and in respect to concentration range. Diagram 5 shows a schematic representation of the individual objects to

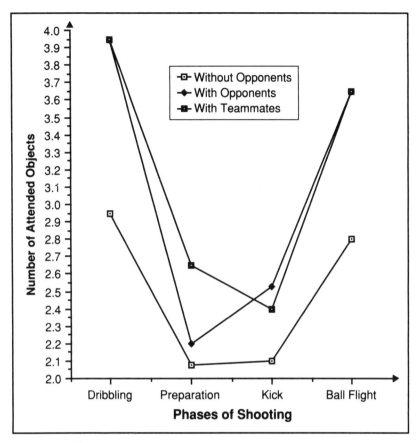

Figure 5   Distribution of attention during shooting on goal attended by goalkeeper in soccer – player in motion.

be observed during the various stages of shooting in each of the team sports. These objects may serve as guides for training methods.

3. Distributive and Focused Attention Test

The Distributive and Focused Attention Test was developed to differentiate between test subjects on the basis of their ability to distribute or focus attention. This test includes performance demands that allow for a comparison between

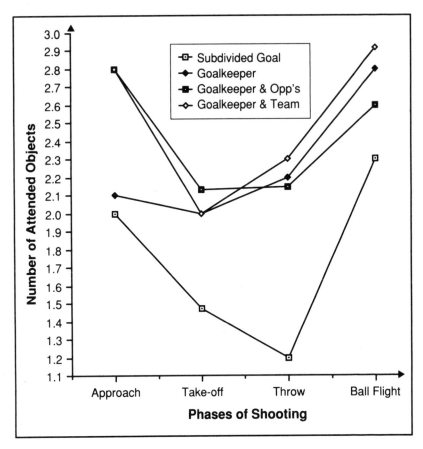

Figure 6   Distribution of attention during throws on goal in handball –
player in motion.

measurable single task and multiple task performances. It is also possible to use
the difference between both results as a criterion for concentration range. Simple
mental tasks, such as calculation and reaction time performance are used.

Our premise was that various types of reactions play a decisive role in
athletic activity and are heavily influenced by attention. These reactions are
especially appropriate performance criteria for identifying specific characteristics of attention, such as focused (narrow) and distributive (broad), while being
influenced by various demands. For this test laboratory conditions were created

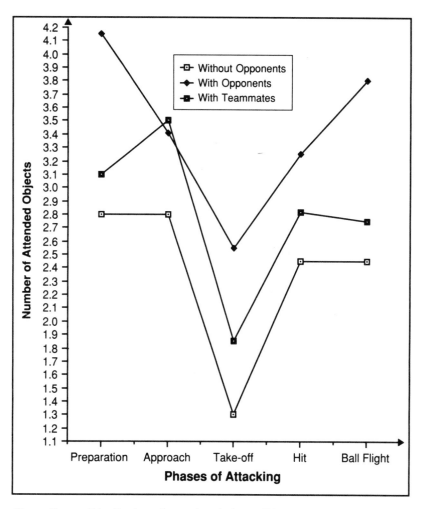

Figure 7   Distribution of attention during spiking in volleyball.

which would parallel athletic activity. The lab conditions can be reproduced, kept constant, or varied methodically. Results are directly measurable. This procedure was developed according to the principle of multiple or double work. The principle requires that the subject perform two activities at once, for example, adding one digit numbers while, at the same time, reacting with a simple motor movement task (i.e., pressing a button with hand or foot) to specific

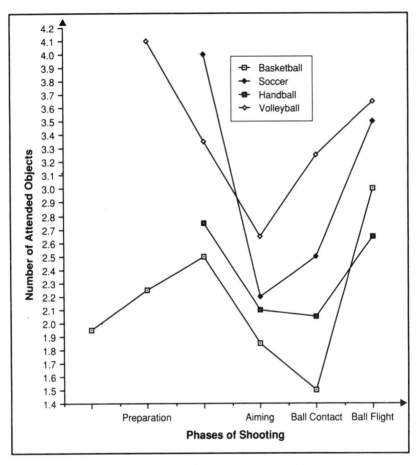

Figure 8   Distribution of attention in four team activities during shooting
            – player in motion.

acoustical, optical, tactile, or mixed signals. A comparison can then be made
between reaction time performance and adding performance under individual
and multiple activity conditions. It is assumed that the subject's ability to
distribute attention is increased the smaller the difference between individual
and multiple task performance results. Conversely, it is also assumed that
focused attention is better developed when a greater difference is found. Any
timing device may be used to measure reaction time, provided that it can be

Table 2 Accuracy of shooting actions in team sports under various conditions (scoring success measured in percent).

Conditions	Basketball 40 Shots on Basket		Soccer 10 Shots on Goal		Handball 16 Shots on Goal	
	Standing Condition	Moving Condition	Standing Condition	Moving Condition	Standing Condition	Moving Condition
	n=400	n=400	n=100	n=100	n=160	n=160
Subdivided Goal/ No Defender	40.4	86.8	47.0	-	87.5	81.2
Goalkeeper	-	-	45.0	58.0	62.0	62.0
Opponents and Goalkeeper	35.0	57.8	15.0	40.0	-	48.8
Teammates and Goalkeeper	33.8	71.2	19.0	40.0	49.0	53.1

linked to the corresponding subject and is accurate to 1/100 s. In the interests of objectivity and accuracy, an attempt should be made to obtain a completely automatic electronic impulse transmission and measurement as well as a computerized printed record of the results. The Multi-Reaction Time Tester (MRTT) developed by Sehner/Nieke/Konzag (Figure 9) was found to be very useful in these experiments. It generates three types of stimulation. The optical signal is given by two lights (right, left), the acoustic signal by two blasts of a horn (right, left), and the tactile signal by two magnets that apply pressure to the skin of the left or right wrist or ankle.

The results obtained from both parts of the test performed as a simple task are needed as an initial basis for comparison. Each series of experiments lasts 90 seconds. During the calculation task series the subject must add one digit numbers as quickly and accurately as possible. The total number of accurately completed calculations represents the subject's calculation task performance.

The mental task test series is followed by the simple reaction task test series, with 15 signals coming at random intervals. These tasks are carried out for each of the three modes of stimulation: visual, audio, and tactile (see Table 3).

The single task experiment is followed by multiple task series where subjects perform mental tasks (calculations) while simultaneously reacting to signals coming either from the right or the left side.

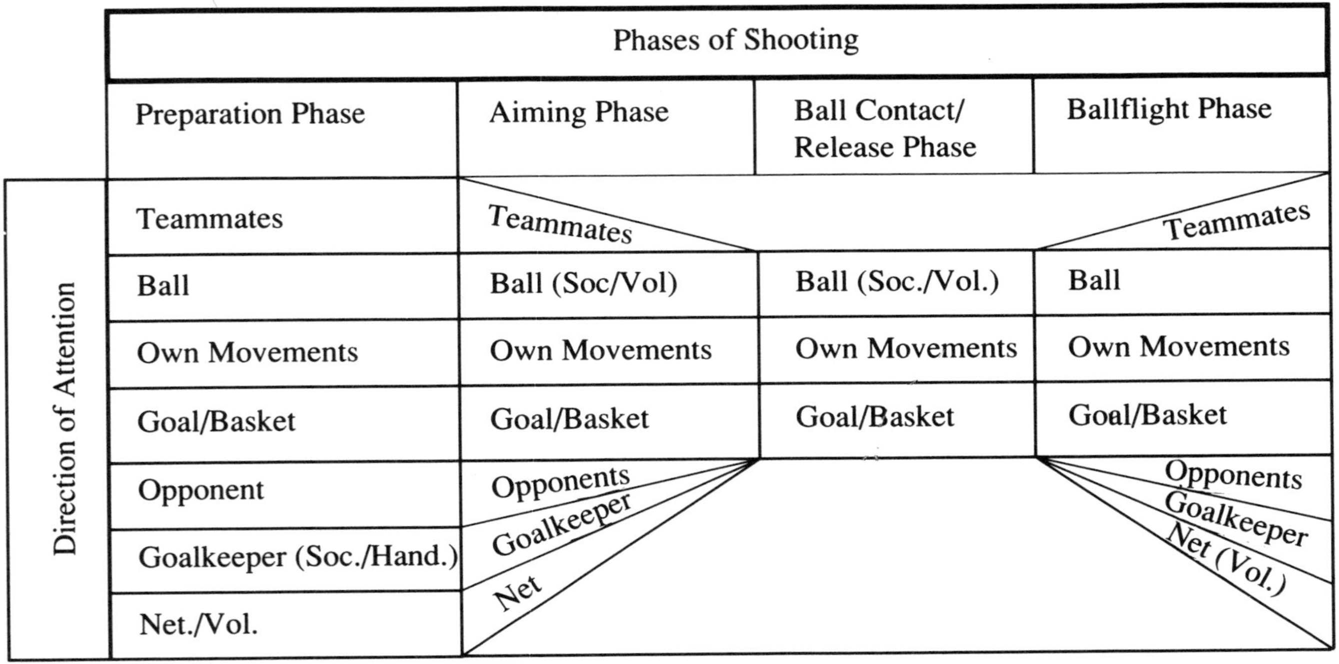

Direction of Attention	Preparation Phase	Aiming Phase	Ball Contact/Release Phase	Ballflight Phase
Teammates	Teammates	Teammates	Teammates	Teammates
Goal/Basket	Goal/Basket	Goal/Basket	Goal/Basket	Goal/Basket
Own Movements	Own Movements	Own Movements	Own Movements	Own Movements
Ball	Ball	Ball (Soc/Vol)	Ball (Soc./Vol.)	Ball
Opponent	Opponent	Opponents	Opponents	Opponents
Goalkeeper (Soc./Hand.)	Goalkeeper (Soc./Hand.)	Goalkeeper	Goalkeeper	Goalkeeper
Net./Vol.	Net./Vol.	Net	Net	Net (Vol.)

Diagram 5   An overview of objects which must be observed (attended to) during goal/basket shooting in team sports under special circumstances of narrowing and broadening of attention.

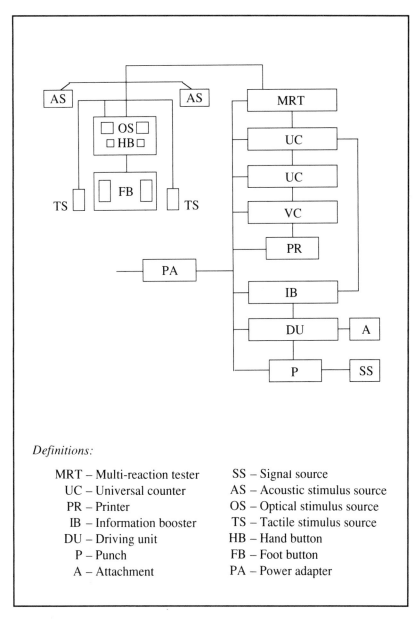

Definitions:

MRT – Multi-reaction tester	SS – Signal source
UC – Universal counter	AS – Acoustic stimulus source
PR – Printer	OS – Optical stimulus source
IB – Information booster	TS – Tactile stimulus source
DU – Driving unit	HB – Hand button
P – Punch	FB – Foot button
A – Attachment	PA – Power adapter

Figure 9   Circuitry diagram of the Multi-Reaction Tester.

The experiments were conducted in the following sequence:

1. Acoustic stimulation—no calculation; reaction to audio stimulus.
2. Acoustic stimulation—calculation; reaction to audio stimulus.
3. Optical stimulation—no calculation; reaction to optical stimulus.
4. Optical stimulation—calculation; reaction to optical stimulus.
5. Tactile stimulation—no calculation; reaction to tactile stimulus.
6. Tactile stimulation—calculation; reaction to tactile stimulus.
7. Mixed stimulation—no calculation; reaction to mixed stimulus.
8. Mixed stimulation—calculation; reaction to mixed stimulus.

In mixed stimulation, acoustic, optical, and tactile signals alternate in random sequence as shown in Table 3.

Table 3   Timing, signal sequence, signal direction and signal mode.

Seconds	Acoustic	Optical	Tactile	Mixed	
1.0	left	right	right	right	- acoustic
9.0	left	left	right	right	- optical
14.0	left	left	right	right	- optical
21.0	right	right	left	left	- acoustic
25.0	left	left	left	left	- tactile
34.0	left	right	left	left	- tactile
44.0	right	right	left	left	- optical
50.0	left	right	right	right	- optical
56.0	right	left	left	left	- acoustic
61.0	right	left	right	right	- optical
68.0	right	right	right	right	- tactile
72.0	right	right	left	left	- acoustic
78.0	left	left	left	left	- acoustic
86.0	right	left	right	right	- tactile
90.0	right	left	right	left	- optical

On the basis of the differences in performance results obtained during single task and multiple task actions, a DFA_1 factor is calculated. This factor expresses the degree of distributive attention ability (if a high value is obtained) or focused attention ability (lower value is obtained during simple task action performance). The results of the calculation and reaction tests must be calculated separately. DFA_1 is obtained in the following manner:

$$DFA_1 = RTF + CPF$$

where RTF = reaction time factor,
CPF = calculation performance factor;

$$RTF = \frac{200\ MTRT \times 100}{STRT}$$

where MTRT = $\bar{x}$ multiple task reaction time,

STRT = X single task reaction time;

$$CPF = \frac{MTCP \times 100}{STCP}$$

where   MTCP = multiple task calculation performance,
STCP = single task calculation performance.

With the calculation of a second factor, DFA_2, the value of the reaction test results, as opposed to calculation performance results, increases considerably:

$$DFA_2 = \frac{DFA_1}{\bar{x}\ STRT + \bar{x}\ MTRT}$$

4. Comparison of Levels of Distributive Attention in Team Sport Players with Those of Other Athletes

The first stage of cross-sectional and longitudinal tests were carried out on 717 test subjects in nine different sports and on subjects not active in sports. The procedure developed to analyze distributive and focused attention (DFA) was utilized. The results based on DFA_1 were as follows:

1. Athletes demonstrate a high level of distributive and focused attention ability specific to sports. Deviations from average levels, when players are required to meet the specific requirements of a particular sport, can be explained in two ways. Sports with high demands on focused attention but low demands

Table 4   Ranking norms for distributive attention (DFA$_1$) ability.

Age Category	n	Very Low	Low	Average	Good	Very Good
10/11	87	under 110	110-129	130-159	160-169	170 +
12/13	167	under 110	110-129	130-159	160-179	180 +
14/15	103	under 110	110-129	130-149	150-179	180 +
16 and up	360	under 110	110-129	130-159	160-179	180 +
Group Total	717	under 110	110-129	130-159	160-179	180 +

Table 5   Ranking norms for distributive attention (DFA$_2$) ability.

Age Category	n	Very Low	Low	Average	Good	Very Good
10/11	87	under 120	120-149	150-179	180-199	200 +
12/13	167	under 140	140-179	180-219	220-249	250 +
14/15	103	under 140	140-189	190-229	230-259	260 +
16 and up	360	under 160	160-199	200-239	240-279	280 +

on distributive attention (e.g., apparatus gymnastics, combat sports, track and field), have a favourable influence on the development of focused attention. Group averages of focused attention for these sport groups are average to good, while levels of distributive attention are low.

2. Sports which place great demands on distributive attention (team sports) aid in the development of this ability. Group averages of distributive attention for these sports are average to good, while levels of focused attention are low (Figure 10). The discrepancy becomes even more apparent when the DFA$_1$ mean values across the four types of stimulation for each of the sports studied are compared. It can be determined that for all test subjects, regardless of the specific nature of the sport the lowest DFA$_1$ values are obtained in acoustic stimulation. The highest values are found in tactile stimulation for all sports with the exception of track and field, where mixed stimulation is the highest. The greatest

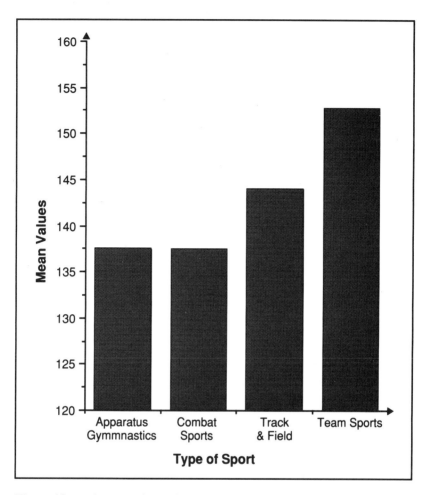

Figure 10   A comparison of DFA 1 mean values across four sports activities.

differences between the sport groups are found in optical and mixed stimulation, where team sport players exhibit the highest levels. This calls particular attention to the importance of both these factors in team sport performance (Table 6, Figure 11).

3.   Females have been found to have significantly better distributive attention

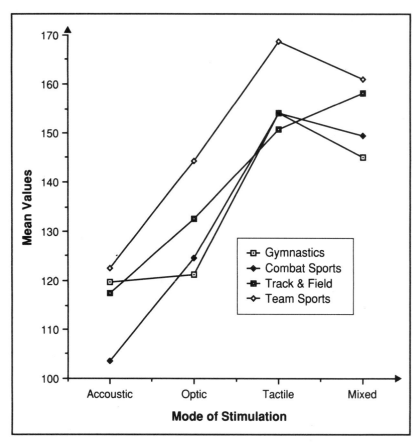

Figure 11   A graphic comparison of DFA$_1$ mean values across four sports activities and modes of stimulation.

and lower focused attention than male athletes in the same sport.

4. Team players with higher distributive attention achieve better results in team sports because they are better able to handle the differences in optical, tactile, and mixed stimulation. This is evident from their shorter reaction and decision-making times, when mental tasks are present.

5. Intelligence (grades at school) does not affect distributive and focused attention ability.

6. The different levels of distributive and focused attention in players is partly

Table 6   DFA$_1$ mean values across four modes of stimulation and four sports activities.

Sport/ Sport Group	n	Acoustic	Optic	Tactile	Mixed
Gymnastics	26	119.8	121.4	154.0	145.0
Compat Sports	75	103.6	124.7	154.2	149.4
Track and Field	41	117.5	132.6	150.8	158.2
Team Sports	134	122.6	144.4	168.7	161.0

inherent and partly environmentally determined. The levels of development of both factors can be improved by objective (sport-specific) and subjective (coach, training structure) targeted training, as well as by competition.

7.   In order to classify and evaluate the individual test results, it was necessary to devise a reference system i.e., norms which would ensure the diagnostic efficiency of the procedure used in comparing the results. Using a standard procedure, DFA$_1$ and DFA$_2$ factors were calculated for the various age categories and for the group in general (Tables 4 and 5). Only minor differences in results across the age groups were found for factor DFA$_1$. We therefore deemed it warranted to use the group's total as a norm for all ages. The results for the second factor DFA$_2$ showed, on the other hand, considerable differences across age groups.

The individual development levels of both factors, as measured by the Distributive and Focused Attention Test, are pertinent for individual assessment of athletes' performance. The development level of athletes' distributive and focused attention, here classified into five categories, constitutes both a starting point for methodical training and a partial contribution towards the establishment of a more comprehensive evaluation of performance requirements for particular sports.

CHAPTER 4

Motor Speed in Soccer with Respect to Decision-Making Processes

1. Introduction

In order to tap the technical and tactical reserves of team players in performance, it is necessary to identify and analyse the operative mechanisms central to game plays, so that they can be put to full use in the training process. The identification of important psychological functions influencing decision-making in team sports is a fundamental challenge to the discipline of sport psychology.

The specific demands made on psychological functions are derived from the multiple reference system (shown in Diagram 6) in which athletes perform. This system is the source of tactical determination for all game plays; it is characterized by rapid and continually changing game situations, situations which make great physical and highly complex psychological demands on players. For this reason, cognitive processes and characteristics are especially required in athletic ability, in addition to drive, emotion, and volition. An analysis of the standards given in this system presumes a continual process of information reception, assimilation, and storage as well as an assessment of the execution. These processes are realized particularly by means of sensations, perceptions, memory, mental images, and thought processes, the quality of which is governed by concentration (3; 10:1103).

Decision-making ability plays a critical role in these functions. We know that every conscious movement, as a link between thought and action, is preceded by a decision (2:298). Making a decision narrows the alternatives for action down to one (16:21). In team sports, decisions in offensive and defensive plays must be made according to the situation since the goals of each action are not fixed prior to the beginning of play. These decisions must be continually reshaped by players during the course of competition. This must be done in conjunction with their teammates' plays, movements of the ball, position in relation to the goal (basket, net) and the actions of opponents who interfere with or block the actions of other players. Because of the large playing area, players have many possibilities for action. These possibilities are restricted by playing

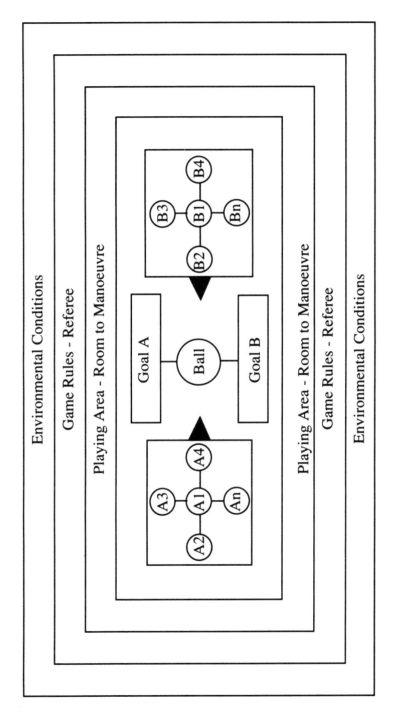

Diagram 6　　Player's multiple reference system.

Players must decide on the best possible action in the shortest amount of time and execute that action quickly and accurately.

field markers, playing time, and game rules. Players must decide on the best possible action in the shortest amount of time and execute that action quickly and accurately. The accuracy and speed of the decision being made during an action influence the action's quality and outcome. The time required for successful decision-making by a player is independent of the overall action.

Although it is possible using symbols to represent the tasks to be solved to verify the temporal range and accuracy of decision-making independent of motor execution in a laboratory test, a similar attempt to verify those decisions for a plan of action during the game will fail. An exact and immediate determination during the competition itself would be the ideal, but from a practical point of view this is not possible. Even experiments under direct field conditions meet with technical problems in measurement and procedures, since it is impossible to keep situation variance to an acceptable minimum.

We have therefore developed a laboratory test in which players must solve a complex but relatively easy task specific to team sports, under conditions which can be accurately reproduced and which imitate field conditions as closely as possible. This test employs the Reaction-Movement Speed Test Apparatus. It measures players' ability to complete the action accurately, in the shortest amount of time. The test taxes the subject's visual perception, concentration, decision-making, reaction ability, and motor speed, all of which influence performance in soccer. Soccer players must possess these abilities in similar or much more complicated situations.

2. Reaction-Movement Speed Test

The Reaction-Movement Speed Test Apparatus (RMST) was designed specifically for soccer players, but with slight variations it can be adapted for use in other team sports (Figure 12). It records the speed at which soccer-specific actions are accurately carried out, with and without a ball, and with and without demands on decision-making and plan of action. Reaction-movement time is measured electronically up to one-hundreth of a second. Aiming inaccuracy and mistakes in decision-making for a course of action are also recorded.

The RMST apparatus consists of a starting mat and a steel frame, to which 4 contact plates (30 cm X 30 cm) with glow lamps and ball targets are attached. The contact plates and the starting mat are attached to the operating control panel with timers.

In this test, subjects are given a total of 5 series of tasks during which they must respond as quickly as possible to each of the 16 optical signals shown in random sequence with fixed motor variations appropriate to the situation. Stimuli are presented by preheated lamps which light up behind fixed contact target plates protected by plexiglass. During this time, electronic time measurement takes place. Each plate must be hit with the inside of the foot or with the ball (inside of the foot kick) from a distance of 1 metre, depending on the task of the test series. The timer is stopped when contact with the plate is made. The task must be carried out accurately i.e., hit designated area of the plate (aiming accuracy) in the direction prescribed i.e., contact correct plate (aiming decision) and according to fixed sequence of movements i.e., using correctly either right or left foot (decision regarding plan of action) as quickly as possible (motor speed).

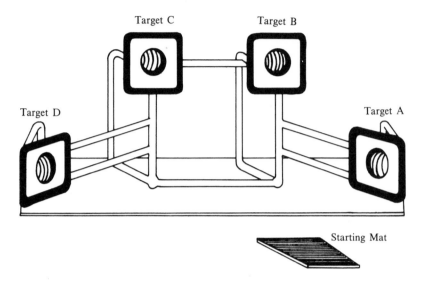

Target C   Target B

Target D

Target A

Starting Mat

Figure 12   The Reaction-Movement Speed Test apparatus.

Below, the five test conditions are described:

Test Condition 1   Without ball/no decision-making/corresponding side.
The subject knows beforehand which lamp will light up and what action to take. Each plate lights up four times in a row. The subject must hit the right plate with the inside of the right foot, and the left plate with the inside of the left foot (corresponding sides). The task must always be completed with a step in between.

Test Condition 2   Without ball/with decision-making/corresponding side.
Rules for movement (corresponding sides) remain the same as above; however, the test subject does not know which lamp will present the stimulus. For this reason, the target direction and the specified motor action must be decided on after the presentation of the stimulus light.

Test Condition 3   With ball/no decision-making/corresponding side.
According to the motor programme to be carried out by the test subject, the target must be hit with the ball kicked with the inside of the foot. To hit the right target the right foot must

Table 7   Protocol of pre-programmed test conditions on the Reaction-Movement Speed Test Apparatus.

Test Condition 1 :
   Without ball (no decision-making)
   corresponding sides (right/right - left/left),
   Alternate :   A/D/1   4 times target A
                               4 times target D
                    B/C/1   4 times target B
                               4 times target C

Test Condition 2 :
   Without ball (with decision-making)
   corresponding sides (right/right - left/left),
   Alternate: B/C/2   12 times target B or C (random sequence)
                               4 times target A or C (random sequence)
                              ─────────────────────────────────────
                              + 8 spare trials

Test Condition 3 :
   With ball (no decision-making)
   corresponding sides (right/right - left/left),
   Alternate: A/D/1   4 times target A
                               4 times target D
                    B/C/1   4 times target B
                               4 times target C

Test Condition 4 :
   With ball (with decision-making)
   corresponding sides (right/right - left/left),
   Alternate: B/C/2   12 times target B or C (random sequence)
                    A/C/2   4 times target A or C (random sequence)
                              ─────────────────────────────────────
                              + 8 spare trials

Test Condition 5 :
   With ball (with decision-making)
   opposite sides (right/left - left/right),
   Alternate: A/C/2   12 times target A or C (random sequence)
                    B/C/2   4 times target B or C (random sequence)
                              ─────────────────────────────────────
                              + 8 spare trials

Editors' Note: Additional trials are utilized when incomplete attempts result
(i.e., faults with respect to correct foot to target selection and/or to hit the target).

Table 8   Reaction-movement speed test protocol.

I.D.:   Name: Last Name:
Sport: Test Group: Date:

No.	Test Condition 1	Test Condition 2	Test Condition 3	Test Condition 4	Test Condition 5
	Actions without decisions	Actions with decisions	Actions without decisions	Actions with decisions	Actions with decisions
	without ball	without ball	without ball	with ball	with ball
	corresponding side	corresponding side	corresponding side	corresponding side	opposite side
1					
2					
3					
4					
5					
6					
n					
$\bar{x}$					

be used; to hit the left target the left foot must be used (corresponding sides). As in the first test condition, the subject knows which target plate will light up four times in a row.

Test Condition 4   With ball/with decision-making/corresponding sides.

Rules for movement are the same as in the third series. The test subject does not know which target lamp will present the stimulus.

Test Condition 5   With ball/with decision-making/opposite sides.

Rules for movement are now different from those of the previous measurement series. The ball must be hit against the left target plate using the right foot (inside of the foot kick); the right plate must be hit using the left foot (opposite sides). Subjects do not know in advance which plate will light up; the stimulus is presented randomly.

A summary of the pre-programmed test conditions is presented in Table 7.

Table 9   Norms for reaction-movement speed of boys without demands on decision-making (test conditions 1 & 3).

Age Category	n	Reaction-Movement Speed Performance Scale				
		very good	good	average	poor	very poor
under 10	48	under 0.969	0.970- 1.079	1.080- 1.169	1.170- 1.269	over 1.270
10-12	92	under 0.789	0.790- 0.889	0.890- 0.969	0.970- 1.059	over 1.060
12-14	155	under 0.879	0.880- 0.949	0.950- 1.049	1.050- 1.089	over 1.090
14-16	110	under 0.759	0.760- 0.859	0.860- 0.939	0.940- 0.989	over 0.990
16-18	79	under 0.739	0.740- 0.789	0.790- 0.889	0.890- 0.949	over 0.950
over 18	38	under 0.729	0.730- 0.759	0.760- 0.839	0.840- 0.919	over 0.920

The RMST apparatus presented here is the latest design in a series of prototypes of such equipment. Its advantage lies in the high stability of its target plates (which are subjected to strong impact by the balls) and in its general portability and solid construction. It can be set up quickly and solidly in any room without any special preparations. In addition, its automatic pre-programme control, with a total of 14 variations, enables the test to be carried out quickly and efficiently (approximately 10 minutes per subject). This test is easily conducted with one person and one assistant.

Table 10 Norms for reaction-movement speed of boys with demands on decision-making (test conditions 2 & 4).

Age Category	n	Reaction-Movement Speed Performance Scale				
		very good	good	average	poor	very poor
under 10	48	under 1.379	1.380-1.439	1.440-1.649	1.650-1.859	over 1.860
10-12	92	under 1.239	1.240-1.319	1.320-1.449	1.450-1.559	over 1.560
12-14	155	under 1.179	1.180-1.289	1.290-1.429	1.430-1.609	over 1.610
14-16	110	under 1.019	1.020-1.069	1.070-1.229	1.230-1.349	over 1.350
16-18	79	under 0.879	0.880-0.959	0.960-1.159	1.160-1.269	over 1.270
over 18	38	under 0.859	0.860-0.919	0.920-1.009	1.010-1.155	over 1.160

A laboratory assistant notes and records the times on prepared raw data sheets. He/she also writes down errors indicated by the experimenter conducting the test (ET = error in aiming at target; EP = error in selecting plan of action; Table 8) and resets the clock after each trial.

Each test subject takes several learning trials on the apparatus before the test trials begin, so that the specific task is understood properly and can be mastered before trial measurement starts.

Measurements are processed statistically and recorded on paper tape. Mean values and standard deviations are calculated for each test subject and for the entire test group with the aid of a data processing unit. Each of the five series of measurements is calculated individually; selected series are then combined under various aspects for analysis (with or without ball, with or without decision-making) and are recorded in prepared data sheets. Errors are tallied.

The reliability of the test was determined by using the test/retest method on a random sample of 67 subjects. It was found to be highly reliable.

After extensive testing with male soccer players of all age categories, norms were developed using the Meili (13) method. These are presented in Tables 9 and 10. The norms are then used for classification and evaluation of subjects based on their test results.

3. Summary

The RMST measures the reaction and movement speed and goal accuracy of elementary actions specific to soccer under conditions which simulate those on the field as closely as possible; these actions serve as a model for the complex motor demands made on soccer players. With this test, simple, standardized, and reproducible demands are made on the range, accuracy, and speed of visual perception (since these demands are present in competition, in similar and considerably more complicated forms.) Players must be able to process information quickly during the test and make decisions on the objectives and plan of action for its realization. Simple game situation decisions are thus simulated. The decision-making processes needed here make operative thinking an imperative. Finally, actions must be executed both quickly and accurately, as is the case under pressure in competition.

Because the skills measured in the RMST are so important their identification must take place in training. This has not been done as yet, even with other currently available methods.

The standardized test conditions and the simplicity of operation and evaluation make the RMST useful for a wider application. In addition, test conditions are totally variable and, with slight modifications, can be used for other team sports.

CHAPTER 5

Social-Psychological Methods for Assessing Group Structures Within Teams

1. Social Psychology in Team Sports

New findings in sports psychology are increasingly expanding the body of knowledge in this science. Literature dealing with sports psychology presents socio-psychological problems concerning communication, trust, leadership, group norms, attitudes, and how they affect performance (3;5;7). Social-psychological questions are important to students studying sports psychology. Sports psychologists who are active in sports recognize the effects of social-psychological mechanisms and their often critical influence on performance; they also devote special attention to the social-psychological methods in their diagnostic activity.

Although social-psychological factors in athletic performance are very important in all sports, they appear to be more important in team sports, since the success of team sports is specifically determined by co-operation among the individual players. The social relationships which are established by players during the course of their training and competition are of prime importance in team sports. Interpersonal relationships on teams is the most researched question in publications dealing with socio-psychological problems in sports (4; 6). The methods used in these investigations are essentially those which have been used to analyse group structures in social psychology.

A complex methodological problem often arises when analysing a particular question. Since developing a new approach to studying the specifics of a particular question is a time-consuming, theoretical, methodological, mathematical, and statistical process, an already existing approach is modified and used in the vast majority of cases. For this reason, results obtained from modified procedures must be checked to find out the extent to which they are influenced by inadequate methodology. A few such problems which arise in the implementation of sociometric procedures in team sports will be discussed in the following section.

Attitudes toward the opponent are an important aspect of a team's psychological preparation before the game begins. The significance of these attitudes in this pre-game state can be seen in an analysis of how individual players, or the whole team, overestimate or underestimate the opponent.

2. Partner Selection Test and Group Analysis Procedure

In the past, social relationships in team sports were analysed primarily with the Partner Selection Test (PST) already used by Moreno in sociometry in the 1920's. A modified form, influenced particularly by Vorwerg's publications, became the best known group diagnostic procedure in the German Democratic Republic (GDR), and was widely accepted in sports psychology. Nevertheless, serious objections were raised to the use of the PST, based on both theoretical and methodological grounds. The main objections are:

1. Moreno's idealistic social theory which forms the basis for the methodology of the sociometric test.
2. The high number of group members who are isolated and rejected by the PST. Generally speaking, far fewer members are rejected or isolated in the individual groups.
3. PST results only provide a ranking scale; the exact distances between the individual group members remain unclear.
4. Empirical data obtained with the PST (usually three selections and three rejections by each person) are incomplete; they do not record the intricacies of the social relationships within the group (2:148).

For these reasons then, a new group procedure has been proposed for the analysis of group structures (8). It is called the Group Analysis Procedure. This procedure has considerable advantages over the PST. The information gained from the empirically determined data is more inclusive, as all group members are included in the assessment, not just the three chosen and rejected in the PST. With the use of an intensity scale it becomes possible to obtain data which can be plotted on a ranking scale and allows easy comparisons of all subjects. This methodological conception, which is based on systematic and theoretical considerations and requires that every "group member" consider his relationship with all other group members, is far superior to Moreno's theory of society.

3. Description, Evaluation and Application of the Group Analysis Procedure

Description

With the Group Analysis Procedure (GAP) each group member makes an assessment of his or her relationship with each of the other group members. Quantification is done according to an intensity scale designed by Esser/Foerster (1). It is a seven-stage scale in which subjects verbally characterize how they relate with other players:

very willingly			neither willingly nor unwillingly		very unwillingly	
1	2	3	4	5	6	7

Since social relationships in the group may vary according to positions assigned (specialization of group members), different questions are asked depending on the objective of the experiment. The questionnaire is drawn up in the form of a leaflet. After each question is answered, this section is folded back to prevent any mistakes filling in the next section. A complete list of names is dictated to everyone before the test is begun. The questions selected are listed at the top of the questionnaire. Test subjects record the number corresponding to their opinion of each group member at the far right of the first question. An "x" or a slash is placed in the space containing the test subject's own name. The column with the answer to the first question is then folded back. Test subjects continue answering the rest of the questions in the same manner.

The questions pertain to various aspects of the group activities. The most common questions are related to work or performance, political activities, and social relationships during leisure time. For this the following questionnaire technique should be used as closely as possible: "How willingly would you (e.g., train) with each of your teammates/group members?" (2:153)

The time required for the experiment will vary depending upon the number of questions asked, the size of the team, and the age of the test subjects. Test time for youths aged 16 to 18 with five questions will not exceed 30 minutes. The experiment can be carried out as a group experiment.

Evaluation

The answers to the questionnaires are transferred to a matrix for evaluation. The names (or the corresponding ID numbers) of the test subjects are placed horizontally and vertically in the matrix. The assessments given for each group member are recorded in rows from left to right. The rating which is given to each individual stands out in the columns from the other group members (Table 11). A separate matrix is used for each question.

The results obtained from these assessments are very important in team sports. They express the athlete's social standing within the group. The results of the ratings given by each member are a measure of the respect which the individual has for his group. They make it possible to formulate statements about individual feelings of well-being within the group. This social group ranking is

Table 11   GAP evaluation matrix.

Name	1	2	3	.	.	.	n	$\sum\limits_{i=1}^{m}$	$\bar{x}$	s	R
1	x										
2		x									
3			x								
.				x							
.					x						
.						x					
n							x				
$\sum\limits_{i=1}^{m}$											
$\bar{x}$											
R											

n = number of subjects

$\sum\limits_{i=1}^{m}$ = total sum of values

m = number of increments in the intensity scale

$\bar{x}$ = mean values

S = standard deviation

R = subject's ranking position based on mean values comparison

arrived at by calculating the respective column means on the basis of which the assessment given to each group member can then be read out.

On the basis of standard deviation values it is possible to assess the uniformity of the values both given and received. To better illustrate the results,

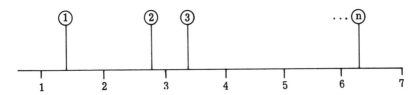

Diagram 7   Graphic presentation of GAP scores on the basis of mean values.

a graph may be used, from which the ranking and mean for each group member (i.e., his social standing) may be determined more clearly. (Diagram 7.)

The results of the GAP may also be evaluated with a data processing unit for which corresponding computer programmes are available (2:155).

For the coach's purposes, a minimal assessment is sufficient in most cases and can be easily made from the matrix. Since the athletes' social positions within the team constitute the prime factor which is to be determined, it is sufficient to calculate the totals, the means, and the rank order.

Application

The results of the GAP allow us to determine the most highly regarded players, the regular team members, and players which are outside of the team.The reasons for the social standing of the individual group members must then be researched with more extensive experiments, discussions and observation. The results must be taken into consideration in training and competition. Players who do not feel a part of the team can be integrated into the group with appropriate measures, such as the assigning of particular tasks for completion. The results are often used to decide on a team captain, to choose members of the Free German Youth (a political youth organization in the GDR), or to decide which players to use in a particular competition.

4.   A Study Using the GAP

Twenty-three male athletes, 16 to 18 years old, were given the following four questions to answer:

1.   How willingly would you play in a deciding competition with each member of your team?

2. How willingly would you spend your free time with each member of your team?
3. How willingly would you participate in political activities (reading newspapers, discussing political problems) with each member of your team?
4. How willingly would you train with each member of your team if your goal is to train intensively?

The first question attempts to give an indication of the social relationships in competition. The second question examines feelings toward other group members. The third question investigates social relationships during political activities discussion. The last question leads to conclusions about the willingness of each team member to train independently.An assessment matrix was drawn up for each of the four questions (Table 12). Only the matrix for the first question is given here; results from the other questions are analogous.

In order to illustrate the results, the values determined from the matrices are presented graphically in Diagram 8. Selected results and implications of the experiment are as follows:

a. Competition Question:
Players 21 and 1 obtained the highest evaluation on the team. Since player 21 is the team captain, his social position as leader is favourable to the team. Athletes 11 and 9 compare quite unfavourably with the team average. They must be integrated into the team by specific educational measures.

b. Leisure Time Question:
Players 21, 16, and 5 were rated highest as leisure time partners. The other team members form a unified whole around the group average. Players 14 and 9 occupy last place.

c. Participation in Political Activities Discussion Question:
Players 5, 16, and 21 at the top are clearly separated from the rest of the players. They are the Free German Youth members and player number 5 is the Free German Youth secretary.

d. Training Intensity Question:
Once again, players 21, 16, and 5 occupy the top positions, with athletes 13 and 7 in last place.

As is evident in Diagram 8, there are a number of players who generally occupy the top positions for all questions, in this case, players 21, 5 and, 16. Others occupy different positions depending on the questions asked, as for

Table 12   Evaluation matrix for competition question.

Number	1	2	3	4	5	6	7	8	9	10
1	x	4	3	1	1	2	1	3	4	1
2	2	x	2	5	1	2	2	3	4	3
3	1	1	x	1	2	4	3	4	5	7
4	1	2	3	x	2	2	3	4	4	1
5	1	1	1	1	x	1	2	1	2	2
6	2	2	3	3	2	x	1	2	4	2
7	1	2	4	2	2	1	x	3	6	1
8	1	2	3	3	2	2	2	x	3	1
9	1	2	2	1	1	1	1	1	x	1
10	1	3	4	3	3	2	2	2	4	x
11	2	4	4	3	1	2	1	3	3	1
12	1	5	4	3	3	2	2	6	4	3
13	2	3	3	2	1	1	1	3	5	3
14	1	3	2	1	2	1	1	1	2	3
15	2	3	4	4	4	3	4	3	4	4
16	1	2	3	1	1	1	2	2	4	2
17	2	1	1	2	1	1	1	2	2	2
18	1	2	2	2	1	2	3	2	2	2
19	1	2	4	3	1	1	4	4	4	2
20	1	1	1	1	1	1	1	1	3	1
21	2	2	3	3	3	3	4	3	4	3
22	2	4	4	3	2	3	3	1	4	2
23	1	1	3	2	1	3	2	2	3	2
Total	30	52	63	50	38	41	46	56	80	49
$\bar{x}$	1.36	2.36	2.86	2.28	1.73	1.86	2.09	2.55	3.64	2.23
s	0.49	1.14	1.04	1.12	0.88	0.89	1.07	1.26	1.05	1.38
R	2.0	13.0	19.0	10.5	3.0	6.0	8.0	15.0	23.0	9.0

$\bar{x}$ (group) = 2.35
s (group) = 0.59

Table 12   Continued

Number	11	12	13	14	15	16	17	18	19	20
1	4	2	2	2	1	1	1	3	3	3
2	4	3	4	3	1	1	1	4	1	1
3	5	3	5	4	2	3	2	4	2	2
4	4	4	2	3	2	2	2	4	4	3
5	3	3	2	2	2	2	2	3	3	2
6	3	2	2	2	2	1	2	3	3	2
7	3	1	1	3	2	2	4	4	4	4
8	4	2	3	2	1	1	2	3	3	2
9	2	2	2	2	1	1	1	1	1	1
10	3	2	3	2	2	1	1	3	3	2
11	x	1	1	2	2	4	3	3	3	1
12	3	x	4	5	2	2	3	4	3	4
13	3	4	x	4	4	3	4	5	3	3
14	2	2	2	x	1	1	2	2	2	2
15	4	3	4	2	x	4	2	3	4	3
16	4	3	3	3	2	x	2	4	2	3
17	2	2	2	3	1	1	x	2	1	1
18	2	1	2	2	2	1	1	x	1	2
19	3	2	3	2	3	1	1	2	x	3
20	2	1	2	2	1	2	1	1	1	x
21	5	4	4	3	2	3	3	4	4	4
22	4	2	3	3	3	1	4	2	3	3
23	4	2	3	3	1	1	1	2	3	2
Total	73	51	59	59	40	39	45	66	57	53
$\bar{x}$	3.32	2.32	2.68	2.68	1.82	1.77	2.04	3.00	2.59	2.41
s	0.95	0.95	1.04	0.84	0.79	1.02	1.04	1.07	1.05	0.96
R	22.0	12.0	17.5	17.5	5.0	4.0	7.0	20.0	16.0	14.0

$\bar{x}$ (group) = 2.35
s (group) = 0.59

Table 12   Continued

Number	21	22	23	Total	x̄	s	R
1	1	3	1	47	2.14	1.13	8.0
2	1	2	2	52	2.36	1.16	12.5
3	1	5	3	69	3.14	1.64	20.5
4	1	5	3	61	2.77	1.15	17.5
5	1	4	2	43	1.96	0.84	6.5
6	2	4	3	52	2.36	0.79	12.0
7	1	4	2	57	2.56	1.4	16.0
8	1	3	3	49	2.23	0.87	9.0
9	1	2	1	29	1.32	0.48	2.0
10	1	2	2	51	2.36	0.89	10.5
11	3	3	3	53	2.41	1.05	14.0
12	1	3	2	69	3.14	1.28	20.5
13	1	3	2	63	2.68	1.21	19.0
14	1	2	2	38	1.73	0.63	4.5
15	1	4	4	73	3.32	0.89	22.5
16	1	3	2	51	2.32	0.99	19.5
17	1	1	1	33	1.48	0.54	3.0
18	1	2	2	38	1.76	0.60	4.5
19	1	4	3	54	2.46	1.14	15.0
20	1	1	1	28	1.27	0.55	1.0
21	x	4	3	73	3.32	0.78	22.5
22	2	x	3	61	2.77	0.92	17.5
23	1	3	x	46	2.09	0.92	7.0

Total	26	67	50
x̄	1.18	3.05	2.27
s	0.50	1.13	0.83
R	1.0	21.0	10.5

x̄ (group) = 2.35
s (group) = 0.59

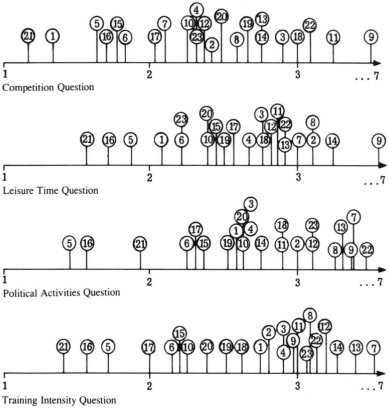

Diagram 8   Ranking positions on the basis of GAP mean scores.

example players 1,7, and 23. Finally there are those players who continually score the lowest (14,11,9, and 22).

5. A Comparison of the Results Obtaine
   in the GAP and the PST

In a second study, 27 male athletes aged 16 to 18 years belonging to a sports team were given the GAP immediately followed by the PST. The question asked for the GAP was *How willingly would you play in a decisive competition with each*

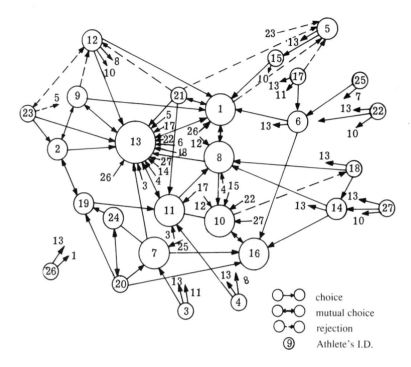

Diagram 9   PST sociogram representing athletes' positive and negative selections.

of your teammates? The question posed in the PST was *With whom from your team would you most like to play in a decisive competition? Why? With whom would you not like to? Why not?* In the PST, athletes were required to name no more than three players. When the players asked if they had to reject certain players, they were told to do so if specifically required by the question. A sociogram drawn up from the results of the PST reveals a clear insight into the make-up of the team (Diagram 9).

Players 13, 1, 8, 10, 16, 11, and 7 form the core of the team, and player 13 with 19 votes clearly occupies the top position. Players 12 and 5 were rejected and are somewhat outside of the group. According to the sociogram, players 3, 4, 15, 17, 18, 23, 25, 26, and 27, are not a part of the group; they appear as outsiders.

A comparison of the GAP and the PST, using the same athletes, is especially

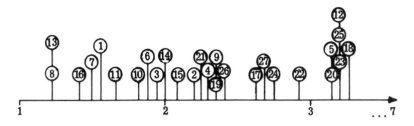

Diagram 10   Means and ranking positions on the basis of GAP competition question scores.

interesting. In the GAP athletes 13, 8, 16, 7, 1, and 17 occupy the top positions in the social ranking order, whereas players 5, 20, 12, 23, 25, and 18 are at the bottom of the scale (Diagram 10). Players 3, 4, 15, and 26, who are classified as outsiders according .to the PST, rank somewhere in the middle of the social ranking order according to the GAP. The formulation of the question in the PST distorts the true ranking position, especially in the middle position of the group. Similar results are found at the end and at the top of the ranking order in both procedures, but the results of the GAP are clearly more accurate than those of the PST.

Upon comparing both methods, it would appear that the GAP makes a more exact determination of the social hierarchy in the group. With the PST, errors in assessment are possible, as is the case with athletes 3 and 15.

These results support the critical objections made to the use of the PST. The results also suggest that the GAP is more appropriate for assessing the social relationships in teams.

6. The Selection of the Team for Competition

An insight into the social relationships among the team members is also of particular interest in setting up the team for competition. Significant findings may be derived from the results of both the GAP and the PST experiments. However, these results are not sufficient for actual selection of the team in every case since the eleven players (in soccer) who may be rated the highest do not often form a team. For instance, too many goalkeepers are often ranked highly. Conversely, too few attacking players receive high rankings. For this reason, final determination of the actual team may be assisted by asking each player to draw up a starting line-up which he thinks has the best chance to win in competition.

The number of entries for each position paints a very vivid picture of the players' attitudes about the team line-up. In many cases, players' choices for filling individual positions correspond completely with those of the coach. Coaches may be confident about the performance of players unanimously picked by all other players. Sometimes, however, several players are named for the same position. In such cases the coach should consider the results of the Group Assessment Procedure. When trust exists between athletes and coaches, the manner in which positions are filled can be discussed openly. Of course, the players do not have the final say in drawing up the ultimate team. This responsibility lies with the coach who must also take into account factors such as specific tactical considerations and specific opponents. In addition, younger players who join the team are rarely named in the ideal team survey. The use of these players should be carefully justified by the coach and carried out in a responsible manner.

In many such experiments, it was determined that the results of a players' survey correspond on average 80 percent of the time with the actual line-up.

Viewed as a whole, this procedure can be considered a highly valuable complement to the social-psychological methods for assessing social relationships within the team. Coaches express great confidence in the results obtained from these surveys.

The Assessment of Team Attitudes
Towards Opponents in Team Sports

1. Difficulties Involved in Determining Attitudes Toward Opponents in Team Sports

Attitude problems take on increasingly greater importance in long-term and immediate preparation for competition as a result of rapid increases in performance and performance frequency.

Publications on attitudes in sports deal mainly with (a) attitudes toward competitive sports and toward sports participation (1; 2; 4;); (b) athletes' ideological attitudes (5); and (c) attitudes toward training methods and training intensity (3).

Until the present time, attitudes toward opponents' strengths have not been subject to investigation in team sports. It is assumed that the attitude of a team toward its opponent and the opponent's actual performance can influence how a team will play. Kossakowski/Lompscher (6) define this attitude toward the opponent as follows: it is an acquired, more or less conscious habitual guidance system for the behaviour of athletes both before and during the game. It is conditioned by athletes' basic beliefs, by team standards, and by current estimations of their own performance strength, as well as the strength of their opponent.

Attitudes toward the opponent are an important aspect of a team's psychological preparation before the game begins. The significance of these attitudes in this pre-game state can be seen in an analysis of how individual players, or the whole team, overestimate or underestimate the opponent. When players overestimate their opponent, they lack self-confidence in their own competitive strength, become unwilling to compete, and consequently make insufficient use of their technical and tactical competitive strength. They are passive and let their opponent's playing tactics become dominant, thereby considerably reducing offensive play. Underestimating the opposing team can result in excessive self-confidence, which will make optimum performance difficult or even impossible. Players play with low concentration levels, believing that they will win without exerting all of their energy, only to be astounded when their opponent turns out to be considerably stronger than was expected. During the course of play, the team is then confronted with the problem of how to change this careless way of playing into a better performance. If this takes too long, or succeeds only partially, team members will become restless. This will detract from the effectiveness of game play, and the outcome will not correspond to the team's optimum performance ability. Overestimating or underestimating the opponent can cause psychological barriers and wreak havoc on the effectiveness of player and team activity (8:234). Attitudes toward the opponent are subject to extremely rapid changes in the current competitive situation. The various kinds of attitudes, the extent to which they prevail, and whether they can be changed during the course of play, is still unclear. This problem is not examined here.

An analysis of players' attitudes toward their opponents provides coaches with information which enables them to influence these attitudes. If players overestimate the opposing team, coaches should build players' self-confidence by placing particular emphasis on the strengths of their own team, as well as on the weaknesses of the opposing team. If players underestimate the opponent, coaches should vividly point out the strengths of the opposing team. These instructions are only guidelines, since the pedagogical and psychological influencing of attitudes toward the opponent always depends on the specific situation of the team and its individual players.

Direct and indirect examinations may be used to determine attitudes toward the opponent. In this investigation, a direct examination of attitudes toward the opponent (e.g., an interview) would be disadvantageous, since there is a danger of distortion in the players' rational estimations of the competitive strength of an opposing team. Therefore, a paper and pencil test was used as an indirect survey in order to determine more accurately the emotional, unconscious components of players'attitudes toward the opponent team.

2. Team Attitude Profile

The Team Attitude Profile used for assessment of attitudes in team sports is based on a method developed by Mathesius (7) for use in competitive sports. It was designed with the purpose of determining psycho-physical states in athletes. This procedure, which was slightly modified for this study, makes it possible to determine players' attitudes toward the physical strength, energy level, morale, and willingness to compete of their own team and of the opposing team.

The attitude of a team towards its opponent can be made more realistic by

Table 13   Team Attitude Profile with factor loadings for the assessment of home team.

Personal Attributes	Bi-polar Variables		Factor Loadings
Physical	(1)	strong-weak	.73
Strength	(4)	powerful-powerless	.53
	(10)	energetic-paralyzed	.64
	(11)	stable-unstable	.50
	(23)	courageous-afraid	.59
Arousal	(9)	tireless-lethargic	.59
	(13)	tense-listless	.67
	(15)	alert-sluggish	.58
	(19)	explosive-lacklustre	.64
	(20)	vigourous-weakened	.72
Morale	(3)	content-miserable	.60
	(6)	cheerful-annoyed	.60
	(14)	satisfied-dejected	.72
	(17)	cheerful-morose	.84
	(18)	happy-distressed	.86

Bracketed numbers refer to the position of the variable in the Team Attitude Profile Inventory shown in Table 15.

encouraging the team to examine critically its own competitive strength. The players' attitudes toward the opponent is heavily influenced by assessment of the competitive strength of their own team. If, for example, a player believes his actual fitness and skill level (technique, tactics, condition, and psychological stability) to be poor, his self-confidence will diminish, and he will judge his opponent in a considerably respectful, more positive manner.

Players must assess the competitive strength of their own team and that of their opponent with the Team Attitude Profile. A comparison of these assessments forms the basis for interpreting the results. A factor analysis performed on the test scores resulted in profiles with partially differing factors and polarities for assessing one's own team and the opposing team.

The Team Attitude Profile for assessing a player's own team contains fifteen bipolar characteristics grouped into three categories designed to assess the major personal attributes in terms of physical strength, energy level, and morale. These characteristics are presented in Table 13. On the other hand, the Team Attitude Profile used for the assessment of the opposing team contains four personal attributes: physical strength, energy level, morale, and willingness to compete (Table 14). Each attribute in both profiles is measured by five bipolar characteristics.

In both profiles morale is evaluated by the same bipolar traits, whereas the other attributes are assessed by different ones. Furthermore, in order to prevent a tendency toward response bias, traits are also arranged in different sequences, and several are reversed. Each bipolar trait is assessed on a seven-point scale, ranging from -3 through 0 to +3. This assessment scale allows a sufficient discrimination in the assessment of attitudes in team sports.

In order to simplify the investigation, the same combined inventory is used for assessing the players' attitudes both toward their own team and the opposing team. This combined inventory is shown in Table 15. Because of the somewhat different composition of the bipolar characteristics for both assessment profiles, however, the values for each are calculated differently taking into account only the relevant traits. The inventory includes three additional characteristics, presumably used as an honesty scale.

3. Application and Evaluation of the Team Attitude Profile

Application

The polarity profile for assessing the attitudes toward the opponent is used two to four days before a game. This period of time guarantees that players are concentrating on their tasks in competition and are preparing, or have already prepared, for their encounter with opponent. In the profile, the player's own team is assessed first, then the opposing team is assessed. Tests last from 5 to 10 minutes. Coaches obtain the results of the experiment immediately after the evaluation is made, and then have the opportunity to influence the team or individual players using pedagogical and psychological methods.

Table 14   Team Attitude Profile with factor loadings for the assessment of the opposing team.

Personal Attributes	Bi-polar Variables		Factor Loadings
Physical	(1)	strong-weak	.60
Strength	(12)	full of energy-tired	.64
	(15)	alert-sluggish	.55
	(19)	explosive-lacklustre	.53
	(20)	vigourous-weakened	.54
Arousal	(4)	powerful-powerless	.55
	(5)	active-passive	.49
	(7)	fresh-dull	.49
	(8)	irrepressible-exhausted	.60
	(10)	energetic-paralyzed	.48
Morale	(3)	lively-sullen	.72
	(6)	cheerful-annoyed	.83
	(14)	satisfied-dejected	.82
	(17)	cheerful-morose	.88
	(18)	happy-distressed	.81
Willingness	(2)	ready to fight-indifferent	.58
to perform	(16)	desire to participate-apathetic	.77
	(21)	fit-worn out	.54
	(22)	ready to increase performance-resigned	.69
	(23)	courageous-afraid	.70

Bracketed numbers refer to the position of the variable in the Team Attitude Profile Inventory shown in Table 15.

Evaluation

For the purpose of analysis the scale values are assigned from 1 to 7, going from positive traits (1) to negative traits (7). For evaluation purposes, means and standard deviations are calculated for each of the 5 pairs of characteristics given

Table 15   Team Attitude Profile Inventory.

Name: Team: Date:

	3	2	1	0	1	2	3	
1. strong								weak
2. indifferent								ready to fight
3. content								miserable
4. powerful								powerless
5. passive								active
6. cheerful								annoyed
7. fresh								dull
8. irrepressible								exhausted
9. lethargic								tireless
10. paralyzed								energetic
11. stable								unstable
12. tired								full of energy
13. satisfied								listless
14. happy								dejected
15. sluggish								alert
16. apathetic								desire to participate
17. cheerful								morose
18. happy								distressed
19. lacklustre								explosive
20. vigourous								weakened
21. fit								worn out
22. ready to increase performance								resigned
23. afraid								courageous

in the assessment of the players' team and the opposing team. The results make it possible to formulate statements about individual players and about the team as a whole.

Graphic Representation and Interpretation of Results

Each player's mean score can be accurately described in graphic form on 1 to 7 point scale. The graphic representation for the assessment of the players' own team is presented in Diagram 11. The diagram is divided according to three attributes for clarity purposes. The results can then easily be interpreted from this graph. When doing so, current expectations of the competitive strength of players' team and of opponents' team are used as a basis. The coach's assessment is used to evaluate and compare the statements made by the players concerning the team and individual players. If considerable deviations from the comparison result, underestimation or overestimation of the opponent is then interpreted. This then allows specific pedagogical and psychological treatment both of individual players and of the entire team. These measures help athletes to develop realistic attitudes toward the opponent and are conducive to performance.

When drawing conclusions from the investigations of the Team Attitude Profile, individual differences among players must be taken into consideration. Using the diagram, coaches can influence those players who deviate considerably from the team average, either positively or negatively, by talking to these players individually before the start of competition. For example, athlete 16 overestimated his own team for all three factors, whereas athlete 21 underestimated his team. Athletes 8 and 12 deviate positively in their assessment of energy level. In terms of morale, athletes 1, 21, 4, and 9 should be given particular attention, as they give their own team a relatively low assessment.

According to the specific situation of a team, closer examination of the attitudes of the leading or top players of the team may be warranted.

4.   Conclusions

The interpretation of the above results has been very superficial. Nevertheless, two conclusions may be drawn from the initial practical application of the Team Attitude Profile.

First, investigations carried out with the Team Attitude Profile up until now have shown that the instrument is appropriate for determining the attitudes of a team and its individual players towards the opponent. These attitudes are

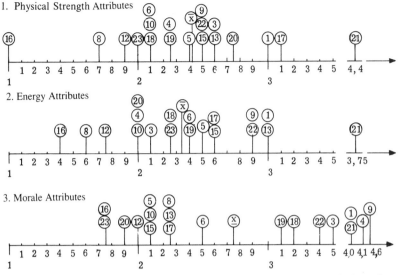

Diagram 11   Assessment of player's home team showing deviations from team's mean values.

classified under personal attributes such as physical strength, energy level, morale, and willingness to compete.

Second, the Team Attitude Profile gives coaches or physical education teachers concrete guidelines on how to influence the team both collectively and individually. This is accomplished through direct pedagogical and psychological preparation for competition and helps develop a positive attitude on the part of players toward both their own team and the opposing team.

Further investigations must examine how to examine attitudes toward opponents by means of other psychological methods. For this reason, a special questionnaire will be designed for the direct examination of players'attitudes.

An important task is to develop methods to build those attitudes toward opponents which are conducive to maximum performance. An effort must also be made to gradually eliminate those attitudes which are detrimental. This may be done by teaching athletes various psychological techniques, such as relaxation training, autogenic training, imagery, etc. Furthermore, specific education of athletes designed to improve their theoretical knowledge about training, strategy, and competition can also be utilized.

Further investigations are therefore very important. Since studying the attitudes toward opponents has always been complex, the approach in this study should aid in the clarification of discrepancies in attitudes during competition in both home games and away games.

Continuing investigations into the problem of attitudes toward opponents in team sports should attempt to make a contribution to the theory of sports psychology regarding athletes' attitudes in competitive sports.

CHAPTER 7 ⚡

Attitudes Toward Competition—
Empirical Investigations in Soccer

1. Factors Which Determine Player Attitudes

According to coaches, athletes, and spectators, player attitudes influence competition significantly. Yet there have been few empirical investigations of player attitudes. In view of this fact, a study was devised to investigate player attitudes in cooperation with a soccer team whose coach and players were preparing for upcoming games.

It is difficult to draw reliable inferences about the nature of attitudes on the basis of direct observation. Hence a survey consisting of twenty-five questions was constructed to which the players could respond directly. Factors presumed to influence players' attitudes towards an upcoming game, such as "my physical condition," team morale," "current standing in the league", and so on, were the focal point of the survey. The players were asked to rank the degree to which their attitudes, in respect to factors such as these, are thought to be positive or a negative influence on the game. A scale from 1 to 7 is used, 7 representing the least positive, and 1, the most positive response. To eliminate any effect that a player's pre-game mental state might have on the results of the survey, and to minimize as well any effect caused by the stress of completing the survey, the survey was conducted one day before the game, after preparation for the match.

The players' answers to survey questions were evaluated and compared. The principle aim of the evaluation and comparison was to understand more clearly the nauture of the factors that influence players' attitudes toward competition and, further, to discover ways in which attitudes might be controlled and ulimately improved.

The survey was administered in three different situations: (1) prior to a game on the road against a team with better record; (2) prior to a home game against an opponent of equal strength; and (3) prior to a home game against an inferior team. The situations may be more precisely defined as follows:

Situation 1 After losing the last two games by a score of 1:2 the team was in ninth place in the league, with 4/8 win/loss record and 13/13 goals differential. Games against the upcoming opponent until then had resulted in 17 losses, 7 wins, and 7 draws. The team had to play without the top player, the regular goalkeeper, and another regular player from the defense.

Situation 2 After the home game against the opponent presumed to be superior ended in a draw, the team was in tenth place in the league, with 5/9 win/loss record and a 14/14 goals differential. The most recent home games against this opponent had ended in a loss. The top player was back, but the injured captain, the regular goalkeeper, and another regular player from the defense had to sit out.

Situation 3 After successfully blocking the last three opponents (7:1, 1:1, 1:1), the team was in eighth position in the league with a 10/14 win/loss record and a 24/21 goals differential. A successful game against an opponent presumed to be inferior seemed possible. All the team's regular players were playing except an injured defender. The anticipated playing conditions were bad: the playing field was frozen solid and covered with a thin layer of snow.

The results are summarized in Table 16. They show noticeable differences in means and in standard deviations across the three game situations.

An examination of differences with the aid of the Mann-Whitney U-test shows only one significant difference; that was the difference between the means from the first and third game situations. No significant differences were found in scores across three playing positions (defense, midfield, and forward positions) and substitute players. Players in different situations did, however, tend to provide quite different evaluations from game to game of the relative importance of various factors affecting their attitudes. In general, the high standard deviation in values may be accounted for by the players' inexperience in dealing with surveys of this type, by the nature of the survey itself—which was both wide ranging in its scope and very complex in its format—and finally by the many different ways in which individual players tended to interpret the survey questions.

The following preliminary conclusions can be drawn from the survey. The team standing in the league before each game influences the values for each of the factors which determine player attitudes. The high degree of agreement among the players across positions suggests the existence of a uniform opinion about the importance of these factors. The reason for this uniformity would appear to be that each survey was carried out after preparation for the game, when the starting line up had already been determined, making it easier for players to orient themselves (2:123).

Table 16   Means and standard deviations of attitudes across various positions in soccer and three testing conditions.

Player Positions	Situation 1 Opponent Superior		Situation 2 Opponent Equal		Situation 3 Opponent Inferior	
	$\bar{x}$	s	$\bar{x}$	s	$\bar{x}$	s
Defense	4.29	2.35	3.37	1.42	3.11	1.65
Midfield	3.93	1.90	3.45	1.64	3.04	1.59
Offense	4.08	2.08	2.88	1.60	2.86	2.07
Substitute	4.06	1.67	3.06	1.75	3.40	1.92
Team total	4.13	2.04	3.21	1.58	3.13	1.60

Information about the significance of each question/item in the questionnaire has been compiled in Table 17. The table summarizes the means, standard deviations, and rank order of the players' responses to the questionnaire. The correlation coefficients for the three rank order sequences indicate a significant difference between situation two and three, but not between any of the other comparisons (game 1 and game 2; game 1 and game 3).

In order to illustrate more clearly the fundamental differences in the values given by athletes before each game, we have classified their answers under four categories. The first category concerns the team; the second, the players' physical and mental states; the third, changing environmental conditions; and the fourth, the opponents. As a further classification, the eight questions that were rated highest on the rating scale, the eight factors rated lowest, and the remaining nine factors which are rated in the middle make up groups A, Z, and N to obtain the values shown in Table 18. This table indicates that before a game, with the exception of situation one, athletes tend to classify team factors the highest, and factors concerning the opponents the lowest.

On average, the athletes surveyed rank second highest, and the most capriciously, those factors which have to do with their individual situation. It seems possible that the reactions of athletes to changes in game conditions are particularly evident here. One cannot overlook the changeable relationship between the players' personal physical fitness and morale, on the one hand, and

Table 17   Means, standard deviations and rank order of questionnaire items.

Factor	Situation 1 Opponent Superior			Situation 2 Opponent Equal			Situation 3 Opponent Inferior		
	$\bar{x}$	s	R	$\bar{x}$	s	R	$\bar{x}$	s	R
1. Tactical conception of our team	3.53	1.88	5.5	2.06	1.16	1.5	1.57	1.09	1.0
2. My physical shape	3.73	2.05	8.0	3.13	1.93	13.5	2.50	1.61	8.5
3. Teamwork and mutual understanding on our team	4.80	1.73	21.0	2.66	1.45	8.0	2.21	1.37	5.0
4. Our opponent	4.66	1.84	19.0	4.27	2.73	21.0	3.93	2.02	19.0
5. Coach's conduct	3.71	≤	7.0	2.87	—	10.5	3.36	—	16.0
6. Success against our opponents up to present	5.20	2.14	22.0	2.13	1.13	3.0	4.00	1.36	20.0
7. Away games play	4.60	—	18.0	4.57	—	24.0	5.00	—	24.0
8. Field conditions	3.00	—	3.0	3.13	—	13.5	5.43	—	25.0
9. Formation of our team	3.53	2.19	5.5	2.27	1.10	4.0	2.57	1.83	10.5
10. Our team's objective	2.20	1.32	1.0	2.40	1.18	5.0	1.86	1.56	3.0
11. My mood	3.86	2.10	12.0	3.47	2.30	16.0	2.50	1.70	8.5

12. Referees	3.43	—	4.0	4.33	≤	22.0	3.71	—	18.0
13. Importance of game to our team	4.06	2.14	14.0	3.40	2.10	15.0	2.29	1.54	6.0
14. Conduct of team management	4.20	—	16.5	3.73	≤	17.0	3.50	≤	17.0
15. Home games	2.27	≤	2.0	2.60	≤	7.0	1.71	≤	2.0
16. Weather	4.13	—	15.0	3.80	≤	18.0	4.93	≤	23.0
17. Our current league standings	6.26	1.18	25.0	4.53	1.88	23.0	2.79	1.12	12.0
18. My task in the game	3.79	1.75	9.0	2.80	1.26	9.0	2.57	1.22	10.5
19. Morale among our team members	4.20	1.93	16.5	3.00	1.15	12.0	2.08	1.14	4.0
20. My immediate opposing player	3.85	1.82	11.0	4.00	0.42	20.0	4.08	1.26	21.0
21. My progress in practice during past weeks	3.80	2.07	10.0	2.87	0.92	10.5	2.36	1.08	7.0
22. Specators	4.00	≤	13.0	3.87	≤	19.0	2.93	≤	14.0
23. Outcome of our last game	5.40	1.84	23.0	2.06	1.58	1.5	2.86	1.61	13.0
24. Physical shape of our team	4.73	2.05	20.0	2.53	1.06	6.0	3.00	1.84	15.0
25. Opponents' play	5.60	1.20	24.0	4.60	1.41	25.0	4.71	2.16	22.0

Table 18   Means, rank order and classification of questionnaire items.

Factor	Situation 1 Opponent Superior			Situation 2 Opponent Equal			Situation 3 Opponent Inferior		
	$\bar{x}$	Ro	Gr.	$\bar{x}$	Ro	Gr.	$\bar{x}$	Ro	Gr.
15. Home game	2.27	2.0	A	2.60	7.0	A	1.71	2.0	A
8. Field Conditions	3.00	3.0	A	3.13	13.5	N	5.43	25.0	Z
5. Coach's conduct	3.71	7.0	A	2.87	10.5	N	3.36	16.0	N
14. Conduct of team management	4.20	16.5	N	3.73	17.0	N	3.50	17.0	N
12. Referees	3.43	4.0	A	4.33	22.0	Z	3.71	18.0	Z
22. Spectators	4.00	13.0	N	3.87	19.0	Z	2.93	14.0	N
23. Outcome of our last game	5.40	23.0	Z	2.06	1.5	A	2.86	13.0	N
17. Our current league standing	6.26	25.0	Z	4.53	23.0	Z	2.79	12.0	N
16. Weather	4.13	15.0	N	3.80	18.0	Z	4.93	23.0	Z
7. Away games play	4.60	18.0	Z	4.57	24.0	Z	5.00	24.0	Z
6. Success against our opponents up to present	5.20	22.0	Z	2.13	3.0	A	4.00	20.0	Z
20. My immediate opposing player	3.85	11.0	N	4.00	20.0	Z	4.08	21.0	Z

Item	Mean	Rank		Mean	Rank		Mean	Rank	
25. Opponents' play	5.60	24.0	Z	4.60	25.0	Z	4.71	22.0	Z
4. Our opponent	4.66	19.0	Z	4.27	21.0	Z	3.93	19.0	Z
10. Our team's objective	2.20	1.0	A	2.40	5.0	A	1.86	3.0	A
1. Tactical conception of our team	3.53	5.5	A	2.06	1.5	A	2.57	1.0	A
9. Formation of our team	3.53	5.5	A	2.27	4.0	A	2.57	10.5	N
3. Teamwork and mutual understanding of our team	4.80	21.0	Z	2.66	8.0	A	2.15	5.0	A
24. Physical shape of our team	4.73	20.0	Z	2.53	6.0	A	3.00	15.0	N
19. Morale among our team members	4.20	16.5	N	3.00	12.0	N	2.08	4.0	A
13. Importance of game to our team	4.03	14.0	N	3.40	15.0	N	2.29	6.0	A
2. My physical shape	3.73	8.0	A	3.13	13.5	N	2.50	8.5	A
11. My mood	3.86	12.0	N	3.47	16.0	N	2.50	8.5	A
21. My progress in practice during past weeks	3.80	10.0	N	2.87	10.5	N	2.36	7.0	A
18. My task in the game	3.79	9.0	N	2.80	9.0	N	2.57	10.5	N

the physical shape and morale of the team as a whole, on the other hand. It would seem that this relationship is not without its own contradictions.

In contrast to the other three groups of items, questions concerning various environmental situations are not valued very differently from game to game. A statistical comparison, however, is misleading since environmental situations vary significantly from one game to the next. The greatest fluctuations in values are noticeable when there is a deterioration of weather and field conditions, and/ or an improvement of the team's standing in the league.

The athletes' evaluations of factors which determine attitudes provide us with a very accurate picture of the state of the team before each game and, according to the data collected, meet the expectations which are associated by soccer experts with identical or similar team situations. This leads us to conclude that the athletes' evaluations are a product of attitudes which they have developed during soccer training and competition, and that the factors which determine attitudes are, in turn, determined by these prior attitudes. Uniform and predictable attitudes can be advantageous to competition; but where such attitudes become stereotyped in an inflexible and unchangeable way, they may become extremely disadvantageous. In competing against a formidable opponent, for example, or an opponent who is unpredictable in game play, a marked change or adjustment in what has become a stereotypical attitude may be required (2:123).

The coach and team must critically examine stereotypical attitudes, encouraging those attitudes which favour cooperation, performance, and personality development, and discouraging those attitudes which work against these tendencies. Two examples may help to clarify this general principle.

1. The relationship between the evaluation of individual players' physical condition and morale and the condition and morale of the team: This relationship varies from game to game according to the team's standing before each game and uncertainties among individual players as to their competence to assess themselves and the team as a whole. Uncertainties such as these can cause individual players to overrate themselves or to rely too heavily on their teammates.

2. It will interest coaches to know that players consider the objective of the game, the tactical game plan, and also, to some extent, the starting lineup of the team to be factors which determine attitudes. If these observations are correct, coaches will be advised to discuss the appropriate objectives and corresponding tactical plans with the players in great detail. Winning the game should never be the only objective, especially where young athletes are concerned. The development of detailed proposals to improve athletic performance and to promote all-

Fitness makes possible high levels of direct intervention and competitive eagerness. In addition, it stabilizes variable teamwork levels and increases the pace of the game.

round individual and team performance is also important.

The survey achieves its intention—to investigate the attitudes of athletes to an upcoming game—but in what is at best only a preliminary way. Nevertheless, it will be appreciated that even though a preliminary study, it brings to light new information and new considerations that may be of value to coaches, and to athletes as well, who are interested in the role played by attitude in sports psychology.

2. Players' and Coaches' Evaluation of theTeam's Game Structure

In general,athletes have not been actively included in the assessment and evaluation of game play on a sufficiently wide scale (1:270-277). Because of the problems which confront soccer coaches and physical education teachers in evaluating game play, the athletes in this study have been given the opportunity to actively participate in the evaluation of the game. Of course, increasing the level of participation by athletes can not by itself solve all the problems;

Table 19   Team's game structure during an away game (first leg) against opponent perceived to be superior by coaches, players and the team as a whole.

Game Structure	Coaches	Attacking Players	Midfield Players	Defensive Players	Team $\bar{x}$
Game trend	3.80	2.30	2.80	3.16	2.78
Teamwork	2.95	2.03	2.60	2.58	2.40
Techniques/tactics	3.88	2.40	3.07	3.30	2.94
Game pace	3.08	2.18	2.93	2.84	2.65
Physical fitness	2.45	1.75	2.47	2.38	2.19

Table 20   Team's game structure during home game (first leg) against opponent presumed to be equal by coaches, players, and the team as a whole.

Game Structure	Coaches	Attacking Players	Midfield Players	Defensive Players	Team $\bar{x}$
Game trend	3.93	4.47	3.83	3.86	4.00
Teamwork	4.03	4.27	4.05	4.30	4.23
Techniques/tactics	4.30	4.73	4.05	4.12	4.33
Game pace	3.83	4.50	3.38	3.92	4.03
Physical fitness	3.83	3.43	3.90	3.68	3.94

nevertheless, player participation should be seen as, the very least, a necessary condition of the evaluation of the team's game. To accomplish this, a procedure was developed to include the athletes and the coaches in the assessment process of the game structure of the team's play.

An inventory was developed which was tested and improved in close collaboration with athletes and coaches until it met all the necessary scientific criteria. The purpose of the inventory was to enable athletes to evaluate the game structure of their own team and of the opposing team. The game structure is analysed from five points of view: (1) game trend (e.g., offensive-defensive); (2)

Table 21   Team's game structure during a home game (first leg) against opponent perceived to be inferior by coaches, by players and the team as a whole.

Game Structure	Coaches	Attacking Players	Midfield Players	Defensive Players	Team $\overline{x}$
Game trend	2.78	2.13	2.05	2.13	2.10
Teamwork	2.70	1.90	2.18	1.85	2.00
Techniques/tactics	3.08	2.30	2.44	2.45	2.40
Game pace	2.70	1.87	2.00	1.95	1.95
Physical fitness	2.28	1.73	2.02	1.88	1.90

teamwork (e.g., collective-individual); (3) techniques and tactics (e.g., highly variable-static); (4) game pace (e.g., quick-slow); and (5) physical fitness (e.g., strong-weak).Each of these aspects is evaluated by 10 bipolar variables on a seven-point intensity scale.

Each player was made completely familiar with the inventory and the testing procedure, and was able to respond to the questionnaire immediately after the game. An attempt was made to ensure that every participant in the investigation retained as many details as possible from the game, to help to make the judgement as unbiased as possible.

Over the course of one entire competitive season, the structure of six games, three home games, and three away games against opponents presumed to be superior, equal, and inferior in strength were rated by all team members and by the coach. The results of the first three surveys are shown in Tables 19, 20 and 21; and the results of the three return matches are presented in Tables 22, 23, and 24 respectively.

On the basis of the results it was possible to:

1.   record and present graphically the short-term characteristics of game trends, teamwork, techniques/tactics, game pace, and physical fitness from the point of view of coaches, individual players by position, and the team as a whole;

2.   determine particular strengths and weaknesses of the team;

3.   compare and determine the degree of uniformity in evaluations made across various positions of the team and made by the coach;

4.   relate the obtained results to the outcome of the game, to the opponent's

Table 22 Team's game structure during a home game (return match) against opponent perceived to be superior by coaches, players, and the team as a whole.

Game Structure	Coaches	Attacking Players	Midfield Players	Defensive Players	Team x̄
Game trend	3.33	2.43	3.33	2.54	2.82
Teamwork	2.83	2.25	2.90	2.04	2.33
Techniques/tactics	3.35	2.90	3.13	2.48	2.78
Game pace	3.20	2.50	3.00	2.42	2.59
Physical fitness	3.08	2.08	2.80	2.18	2.30

Table 23 Team's game structure during an away game (return match) against opponent perceived to be equal by coaches, players, and the team as a whole.

Game Structure	Coaches	Attacking Players	Midfield Players	Defensive Players	Team x̄
Game trend	3.10	2.75	2.87	2.26	2.58
Teamwork	2.53	2.43	2.90	2.04	2.40
Techniques/tactics	2.90	2.75	2.97	2.22	2.58
Game pace	2.65	2.97	2.77	2.22	2.61
Physical fitness	2.38	2.45	2.43	2.24	2.36

competitive strength, to the objective of one's own team, and to the success or failure of the game structure.

In very general terms the results show that the coaches' and players' (attack, defense, midfield) evaluations of game structure may vary considerably from game to game or may, on the contrary, show a high degree of uniformity. The technical/tactical aspects of game situations constitutes a major weak point in all of the games, except the fifth game. The game trend in all but two games is classified as being just slightly better. The best assessment is given to the

Table 24   Team's game structure during an away game (return match) against opponent perceived to be inferior by coaches, players, and the team as a whole.

Game Structure	Coaches	Attacking Players	Midfield Players	Defensive Players	Team $\bar{x}$
Game trend	2.40	2.15	2.84	2.48	2.52
Teamwork	2.43	2.38	2.98	2.50	2.65
Techniques/tactics	2.79	2.48	3.22	2.75	2.85
Game pace	2.60	2.43	2.88	2.73	2.69
Physical fitness	2.53	2.30	2.90	2.40	2.59

physical fitness aspects in all but the sixth game. Game pace and teamwork, alternately, hold the middle position. (Note that lower numbers represent more positive responses, while higher numbers represent more negative responses on the seven-point scale used in this study.)

In general, a good level of physical fitness is considered to be the decisive factor. Fitness enables the team to compensate partially or totally for obvious technical and tactical shortcomings and for a highly unoriginal game tendency. Fitness makes possible high levels of direct intervention and competitive eagerness. In addition, it stabilizes variable teamwork levels and increases the pace of the game.

The evaluations by coaches, the players (attackers, midfielders, defenders), and by the entire team were examined using the Mann-Whitney U-test. These assessments correspond in some but not all cases. The summary results are described below.

1. Assessments by coaches and the team correspond for the second and sixth games, but deviate significantly for the third and fourth games. Both sets of games are classified much more positively by the team (especially the third game) and by the the attacking and defensive players (especially the fourth game), than by the coaches.
2. Assessments by coaches and individual units of the team correspond for the first .game (coaches, defensive, and midfield players), for the fifth game (coaches, midfield, and attacking players), and for the sixth game (coaches and defensive players). But the assessments deviate significantly from each other for

the first game (coaches assess significantly more negatively than attacking players), for the fifth game (coaches assess significantly more negatively than defensive players), and for the sixth game (coaches assess significantly more negatively than attacking players, and significantly more positively than defensive players).

3. Assessments by the various units of the team correspond completely for the second and third games. A partial correspondence is present for the first game (midfield and defensive players), for the fourth game (defensive and attacking players), and for the fifth game (midfield and attacking players). The assessments deviate significantly after the first game (attacking players assess significantly more positively than midfield and defensive players), for the fourth game (defensive and attacking players assess significantly more positively than midfield players), for the fifth game (defensive players assess significantly more positively than midfield and attacking players), and for the sixth game (defensive and attacking players assess significantly more positively than midfield players).

The possible influence of external conditions on these assessments cannot be discounted or excluded without further investigation. Assessments of the game structure were sometimes uniform, sometimes significantly different. These assessments appear to reflect the discriminative influence exerted by individual units (offence, defence, midfield) of the team on the classification of game structure.

The game structure assessments of each game were compared. The results of this comparison show significant differences between the assessments of the second game and the assessments of the other five games. Even greater differences were shown between the assessments of the third and fourth games. Significant differences between the assessments made by coaches, all units of the team, and the team as a whole are observed in game combinations of games 1, 3, 5, and 6. Non-significant differences are found particularly in the assessments of game combinations of games 1, 4, 5, and 6.

In summary, concerning all fifteen possible game comparisons, the differences in assessments of game structure made by coaches, attacking players, and midfield players are significant in nine cases, and non-significant in six. The assessment comparisons of defensive players are significant in eleven cases and non-significant in four. The assessments of the team as a whole are significant in ten cases, and non-significant in five. In other words, half of the assessments of game structure differ significantly from game to game.

It is commonly said that in soccer every game is different. But on the basis

Table 25   Comparison and ranking between outcome of the game and assessment of the game structure by the coach and the team as a whole.

Opponent	Outcome of Game	Ranking Outcome of Game	Game Structure Assessment Team Coach		Ranking Game Structure Assessment Team Coach	
1.	1:1	5.5	2.59	3.19	4th	5th
2.	1:1	5.5	4.10	4.09	6th	6th
3.	5:0	1st	2.06	2.71	1st	2.5
4.	2:0	3rd	2.57	3.15	3rd	4th
5.	1:0	4th	2.51	2.71	2nd	2.5
6.	3:0	2nd	2.65	2.55	5th	1st

of the above-mentioned, we must conclude that although every game is different, perhaps not every game will be assessed in a significantly different way.

The results of our investigation compel us to examine more closely the relationship between the coaches' and team's assessments of game structure and the outcome of the game, the opponent's competitive strength, the team objective, and the success or failure of the team's game structure. The examination is important not only because it sheds light on the reasons behind our research, but also, and most important of all, because it will tell us something about the influence of the coaches' and the team's assessments.

In further examination of the data, the mean averages based on the coaches' and the team's assessments, and on the outcome of the game, were ranked as shown in Table 25. The ranking correlation coefficient R, as calculated by Krueger-Spearman procedure, yielded no significance at the .05 level in terms of the relationship between the rankings of "outcome of game" and "assessment of game structure."

Non-significant correlations were found between the ranking sequences for the coaches' and team's assessments of game structure and the ranking sequences of "opponent's competitive strength," "goal of own team," and "success or failure of team's game structure". From these results it was concluded that coaches and athletes base their assessments of the game structure heavily upon the game activity itself. We stress that this conclusion is only a hypothesis, and can be supported only by excluding other possible influencing conditions.

In summary, our questionnaires enable players to analyse their impressions of the game in a manner that is concrete and demonstrable. That makes the impressions and observations of athletes and their coaches objective, quantifiable, and readily accessible to interpretation. Among these data were detailed classifications of game structure which made possible a reliable presentation of the important elements of the game and of a team's strengths and weaknesses. Coaches will be able to use this initial data to evaluate the game, to improve training, and to organize the educational process.

Comparisons between the assessments of game structure done by coaches, the three units of the team, and the team as a whole after each game give us an insight into the conditions which influence these assessments.

3. Players' and Coaches' Evaluation of the Opponent's Game Structure

Further research into players' attitudes was undertaken to study their attitudes towards the opposing team. A second inventory was developed to evaluate the opponents' game structure. It was subdivided into the following five aspects: "game trend," "game pace," "teamwork," "technique/tactics," and "competitive eagerness." The questionnaire used two types of evaluation, overall and specific. The overall evaluation simply asks the players to evaluate the opposing team on one question. The question reads: *The opposing team as compared to our team is* _____ . The possible responses use a seven-point scale as follows: superior in all respects (1), superior (2), partially superior (3), equal (4), partially inferior (5), inferior (6), and inferior in all respects (7). The specific evaluation, on the other hand, uses six bipolar variables (e.g., offensive-defensive) for each aspect of the game structure, thus yielding a questionnaire that addresses 30 items. Each variable is evaluated on a seven-point intensity scale.

The double assessment which coaches and athletes are required to make about the opposing team's game structure should provide the basis for a rough comparison between the opposing team and one's own team, and should reveal particular aspects, strengths, and weaknesses believed by athletes and the coach to be typical of the opposing team.

The specific expectations of this phase of research were: (a) to achieve identical or similar assessments of opponents of equal strength and different assessments of opponents of different strength and (b) to provide an insight into the degree of uniformity of assessments of players and of coaches.

The investigation was carried out a few days before the beginning of the second half of league play. After a briefing on the procedure and its structure, nine athletes and two coaches evaluated the game structure of the first three opponents using the questionnaires. Although the teams of the first and second opponents were ranked as superior to the home team in some respects, they were perceived as being equal to the home team in strength. The first and second opponents were in fourth and third position in the league standings, with a 15/11 and 17/9 win/loss record respectively. The third opponent was equal in strength, but was considered by the home team to be weaker than the first and second opponents. The third opponent was in twelfth position in the league, with a 10/16 win/loss record. The home team was in sixth position in the league with 15/11 standing. Detailed assessment results will be presented and discussed only for the second opponent (Table 26); Table 27 will present summary results for all three assessments.

The results in Table 26 present the values for the overall evaluations and the mean averages for the specific evaluations of the second opponent's (third place in the league) game structure, as provided by athletes and coaches. In comparison, the overall evaluation scores are significantly higher (U-test analysis) than the corresponding values for the specific evaluation (i.e., mean scores below the 4.0 neutral point). The exceptions include athlete 4, aspects 1 and 3, and athlete 3, aspect 4. Furthermore, statistical analysis indicates that the mean values in the overall evaluation for the first four aspects deviate only slightly from each other, but do deviate significantly from the value for the fifth aspect. The slight differences in the values for the specific assessments of the five aspects of game structure are non-significant. In all assessments (coaches and athletes), variations about the mean are low, ranging from 0.23 to 0.95, indicating that the assessment of the opponent's game structure is uniform across athletes and coaches.

On the basis of the overall evaluation this team is, on the whole, perceived equal to, and in some respects superior to, the opposing team. It is perceived equal in respect to competitive eagerness, but slightly superior in respect to other aspects of game structure, i.e., teamwork, game trend, game pace, and technique/tactics.

On the basis of the specific evaluation, the opposing team is viewed as superior in respect to all aspects of the game structure, but particularly in respect to game pace and techniques/tactics. Players on the home team evaluated their opponents as being controlled, effective, expansive, quick, strong in one-on-ones, and daring, but at the same time, as being "more unfair than fair."

Table 27 provides an evaluation summary of the means for the coaches' and athletes' overall and specific assessments for all three opposing teams.

Table 26 Coaches' and players' evaluation of the second opponent's (superior opponent ranked third in the league standing) game structure.

Athlete	Game Trend		Game Pace		Teamwork		Techniques/ Tactics		Competitive Eagerness		Overall Mean	
	O*	S**	O	S	O	S	O	S	O	S	O	S
1	4.00	3.17	4.00	2.50	4.00	2.83	4.40	1.83	4.00	3.17	4.08	2.70
2	3.60	3.00	3.60	1.87	3.60	2.17	4.00	2.17	4.00	2.33	3.76	2.31
3	3.00	2.67	3.60	2.67	4.00	3.33	2.40	2.50	5.00	2.33	3.60	2.90
4	3.00	3.17	3.40	3.00	3.20	3.33	4.00	3.33	4.40	3.33	3.60	3.23
5	4.00	3.00	3.00	2.50	3.40	3.17	4.00	2.83	4.00	3.50	3.68	3.00
6	3.60	2.83	3.40	2.17	3.40	2.67	3.80	2.83	4.00	2.33	3.64	2.57
7	4.00	2.83	3.80	2.83	3.80	3.00	3.40	2.17	4.20	2.67	3.84	2.70
8	4.00	3.17	4.00	3.67	3.60	3.17	4.00	3.50	4.00	3.33	3.92	3.37
9	3.00	2.33	3.60	2.00	3.00	2.50	3.00	2.33	4.00	2.50	3.32	2.33
x̄=	3.58	2.91	3.60	2.58	3.56	2.91	3.67	2.61	4.18	2.94	3.72	2.79
Coach 1	3.60	3.33	4.00	2.50	4.00	3.00	3.60	3.17	4.60	2.67	3.96	2.93
Coach 2	3.40	2.87	4.00	2.67	3.60	3.00	3.80	2.67	4.60	3.17	3.88	2.88
*=	3.50	3.10	4.00	2.59	3.80	3.00	3.70	2.92	4.60	2.92	3.92	2.90

* O - overall evaluation   ** S - specific evaluation

Opponent	Athlete Coach	Game Trend O S	Game Pace O S
1st	athlete	2.91-2.76	3.51-2.33
	coach	3.00-2.92	3.80-2.17
2nd	athlete	3.58-2.91	3.60-2.58
	coach	3.50-3.10	4.00-2.59
3rd	athlete	4.64-3.69	4.49-3.30
	coach	4.20-3.25	4.40-3.00

Teamwork O S	Techniques/ Tactics O S	Competitive Eagerness O S	Overall Mean O S
3.29-2.50	3.02-2.07	4.18-2.30	3.38-2.44
3.80-2.67	3.20-2.25	4.70-2.50	3.70-2.50
3.56-2.91	3.67-2.61	4.18-2.94	3.72-2.79
3.80-3.00	3.70-2.92	4.60-2.92	3.92-2.90
4.80-4.13	4.38-3.37	4.74-3.31	4.61-3.56

In the overall assessment made by the home team, the first and second opposing team are classified as being equal, to partially superior; the third opposing team, on the other hand, is classified as being equal, to partially inferior. Corresponding assessments made by coaches reveal the same evaluation trends; however, the trends are not as marked. The differences were found to be non-significant using a U-test analysis.

In the specific evaluation, athletes and coaches give significantly different assessments for each of the opposing teams. Of the individual aspects of game structure, techniques/tactics, and game pace of the opposing teams were evaluated as being better than that of the home team. These were followed by competitive eagerness, game tendency, and tactical teamwork. The athletes' and coaches' evaluations corresponded so closely that no significant differences were found with the U-test between the corresponding values.

The large degree of correspondence between the evaluations of the individual players, the team, and coaches forms a reliable basis for drafting a game plan. Those individual assessments that indicate the superiority of the opposing team should become the focal point of these joint considerations. Only when the opposing team is considered in this way is it possible for our team to deal with a quicker game pace and better techniques. If the opposing team finds itself able to display its superior speed and techniques, our team will encounter difficulty.

For this reason, then, the focal point in game preparation should be the development of appropriate measures to counter more successfully the strengths of the opposing team. Players who have particularly different evaluations of the opposing team should be approached individually and given special objectives and instructions.

An evaluation of our research concerning the attitudes of athletes and coaches toward the game structures of opposing teams makes it possible to

1. Draw more attention to the mental conceptions which athletes and coaches have of the game structure of the opposing teams and of their similarities and differences. Even in the case of opponents who are equally matched, no two of these conceptions are the same;

2. Indicate to what extent the individual athletes, the team as a whole, and the coaches agree in their evaluation of opponents. This helps prevent the tendency to overestimate or underestimate an opponent; and

3. Outline the mental conceptions which athletes and coaches have of the game structure of their own team.

The mental images which our athletes and coaches have of the opposing teams reveal notable differences in the particular strengths and weaknesses of opponents who are almost equally matched, as well as of opponents who have very different strengths. We should draw attention to two points in assessing opponents. First, the assessment of the opponents should not be based on their standing in the league; and second, the conspicuous classification of competitive eagerness, especially of the partially superior opponent judged to be equal, should be a point in favour of the self-confidence of the home team. The team, at that time, was judged to be very eager to compete, which allowed it to compensate partially for technical shortcomings. The highest evaluation of all the opposing teams was in the areas of techniques/tactics and game pace. These were the major shortcomings of the home team.

The characteristics which were mentioned are typical of our team and, as a type of group norm, help in the orientation process. The presence of stereotypical attitudes becomes especially apparent, since the assessments of all opposing teams reveal only a slight mean variation, and the judgements made by individual players and coaches correspond to a large extent.

The unanimity in the assessments of our athletes and coaches is, without a doubt, the result of common experience with opposing teams. However, during this process of judgement-making, the adoption of assessments made by coaches, the media, etc., with which our athletes are continually confronted also plays a significant role. Last but not least, a common conception of the expectations of the person conducting the experiment should be taken into consideration as a pre-condition of uniform assessments. The decisive factor here is the way in which the unanimity in the assessments of the opposing team favours our athletes' activity, paves the way toward cooperation and understanding, develops common goals and, by means of joint action, helps realize and fulfil these goals. Research in sports psychology provide fundamental assistance in leadership and decision-making and can be an effective part of the education and training process of our athletes.

CHAPTER 8

Psychological Stress in Team Sports

1. Relationship Between Demands and Stress in Human Activity

Stress is a product of physical and psychological exertion that is present in virtually all human activities. To cite some obvious examples, it is present in play, in most learning processes and work situations, and, indeed, in most—if not all—cognitive activity. Precisely defined, stress is a psycho-physical phenomenon that "leads to a weakening in the psycho-physical state of the individual causing a deterioration in activity or an increase in the psycho-physical exertion necessary per unit of performance." (2:73).

Accordingly then, stress includes the objective external demands of various forms of activity, as well as the subjective manner in which an individual experiences and copes with these demands. It is common knowledge that great physical and psychological demands do not always lead to physical and psychological stress, just as physical and psychological stress do not have to be preceded by correspondingly high levels of physical and psychological demands in every case. Identical external demands will not trigger the same stress reactions in every individual. External stimuli are not experienced as stress until the individual becomes engaged in a subjective retrospective process, with all its diverse and variable conditions. How individuals react to specific external demands depends on the subjective manner in which they meet these demands and on their general physical and psychological capacity to bear stress. People, in the various spheres of their activity, are able to handle relatively high levels of stress. Both work and sports psychology have determined that psychological stress is caused primarily by factors found outside the actual activity negatively influenced by this stress. These factors may include poor health, family conflicts, tension in relationships with colleagues or superiors, inferior working or living conditions, sexual problems, financial worries, feelings of failure, or general communication problems. Such difficulties and problems have a negative effect on the general well-being of an individual and on his/her overall ability to perform. These difficulties also greatly reduce the athlete's ability to bear physical and psychological stress. To preserve overall performance ability and psychohygiene, the science of maintaining psychological and psychosomatic well-being should be given greater attention in our daily lives.

2. Psychological Stress in sports

Specific demands, such as the number of drills, the degree of difficulty, and the length, quality, and intensity of exertion, are continuously made on an athlete during training and competition. In principle, it is not important whether sports are done for general health, therapy, and rehabilitation or for improving fitness through school physical education programs, training in sports clubs, or training for amateur and competitive sports. In sports, as in any other form of human activity, psychological stress is contingent on the external demands that are made on individuals and on the manner in which these demands are experienced internally (subjective retrospection) during a particular sporting activity. The continual growth of athletic performance in all age groups, the continually expanding limits of performance in individual sports, and the narrowing gap between the best athletes in the world make it imperative to deal with the problem of psychological stress in sports: it must be given the appropriate pedagogical and psychological attention in exercising, training, and competition.

Any activity in sports must be completed under concrete conditions, thus making both physical and psychological demands on the athletes. The presence of psychological stress depends on the given activity, on the conditions for its execution, and on the athlete's feelings or inner states (personality traits, needs, interests, attitudes, moods, etc.).

The activity and the conditions for its execution and the athlete's personal state forms the objective and subjective bases respectively for varying levels of psychological stress. The relationship between the objective and subjective bases for psychological stress also plays an important role. Activities or goals which are both personally and socially important to an athlete do not always cause psychological stress and corresponding negative reactions as quickly as the relatively low demands made by goals and activities which are not accepted subjectively. This is especially true in amateur sport and competition where the scope and intensity of demands have become greater. The stress factors outside of sports also have a decisive influence on the execution of athletic activity. The effect of physical and psychological stress factors on athletic ability is treated in the following section.

3. Psychological Stress and its Significance in Team Sports

Demands and Stress in Team Sports

The demands which are made of team players are highly complex and cannot always be generalized. For example, soccer is played in direct confrontation with the opponent, the object being to score as often as possible and to prevent the opponent from scoring. Volleyball, on the other hand, is played without direct opponent contact, and the object in this instance is (1) to hit the ball over the net and into the opponent's playing area so as to prevent the opponent from returning it and (2) where the ball has been successfully returned by the opponent, again to hit the ball back over the net in a way that prevents the opponent from returning it—all of this within the framework of a specific set of rules. As a result of these differences, different physical and psychological demands confront players in training and competition.

According to a dictionary of psychology (2:30), the word "demands" denotes the "total of objective requirements of human activity for the success of a specific task, i.e., the transition from a specific beginning of an activity to a specific and evaluated end, under particular conditions for its completion." Demands in team sports can be the external requirements of coaches, officials, team group, teammates, etc. or the internal requirements of the players' sense of self-discipline and self-perfection. Athletic activity places exceedingly great physical and psychological demands on players who must constantly work towards psychological and physical perfection; they must completely master the techniques involved in using sports equipment (the ball); and they must heed competition rules.

A distinction is usually made between physical and psychological stress, depending on the predominance of muscular or mental activity. In training and competition we have to deal equally with physical and psychological stress, since psychological activity is becoming as important as physical activity, especially in team sports. Stress begins when a player commences training in a group and must align his norms and values with the objectives of the group. The extent to which team players experience psycho-physical stress in training and competition depends on the complexity of social and athletic objectives, conditions for activity execution, relationships of athletes among themselves or with coaches, sports physicians, the extent and difficulty of an activity, and the performance capabilities of the individual players.

In this light, the following three factors of motivation control are of

The extent to which team players experience psycho-physical stress in training and competition depends on the complexity of social and athletic objectives, conditions for activity execution, relationships of athletes among themselves or with coaches, sports physicians, the extent and difficulty of an activity, and the performance capabilities of the individual players.

particular importance in athletic activity:

1. Quality of the cues given by individual players: these are necessary for the rapid recognition of a game situation and for quick, effective decision-making for the particular situation (passing, dribbling, feinting, or shooting on goal).

2. Player attitudes toward social objectives, motivation, willingness to exert oneself, and emotions in particular situations.

3. Physiological and personality characteristics which influence body functions and are coordinated and adapted to environmental conditions.

The demands made on athletes in sports depend on the activity, the athletes' experience, learning of the task, and concrete conditions for execution. It has been proven both in work and sports psychology that as the activity increases in complexity the number of personality systems and system complexes involved in the competition of action increase. As the number of systems and system complexes increases, so too does the likelihood that psychological stress will influuence the outcome of the action.

The objective demands made on team players are a result of the multiple reference system (teammates, opponents, ball, referees, playing field, spectators) with which they must actively come to terms. During the game, players must rapidly and accurately absorb and process constantly changing information under high physical and psychological demands. Great physical demands affect the fitness and coordination of each player in team sports differently than in other sports. Fitness and coordination, along with technique and tactics, are essential for playing against an active opponent. Also important where psychological stress is concerned are offensive and defensive plays requiring decisions appropriate to the situation. Rapid perception, memory, and thought processes are needed for decision-making and are of critical importance to the successful outcome of the game. The object of each game is for players to use the greatest possible number and variety of tactics and motor sequences to solve a particular situation, while ensuring that such activities are completely coordinated in the face of the counter-strategies and tactics of the opposition.

Psychological stress in team sports is the result not only of the various demands of a particular activity, but also of demands which come from outside training and competition. Empirical findings confirmed by active participants, coaches, and sports officials show that competitive ability is often influenced to a greater degree by factors resulting from demands outside training and competition than by factors experienced directly in training and competition. Stress factors in an athlete's daily life may include relationships with family, love life, job, studies, housing, and health. How athletes experience and cope with these stress factors and other psychological stress factors outside sports influences their competitive ability.

Psychological Stress in Team Sports

The demands that have been described in the previous section, whether from athletic activity or daily life, do not necessarily cause psychological stress, since by themselves they do not produce feelings of strain and tension. If athletes are able to cope successfully with the demands that are made on them by maintaining their required psycho-physical levels, without bringing additional systems into play to compensate for the external and internal stimuli, then it is unlikely that stress situations will arise that will affect their competitive ability negatively.

The variety of demands that individual players must face in team sports can be quite wide, depending on player attitudes toward a particular sport activity, on the motivation and individual willingness of players to perform and exert themselves, and on the emotional state of players in particular situations. If, however, an athlete has exceeded his or her individual limit for successfully coping with the demands made and the psycho-physical equilibrium has been disturbed, he or she will experience a subjective state of psychological stress. This generally results in a deterioration of competitive ability in sports and makes necessary a considerable increase in the strength required for achieving the desired result.

Psychological stress becomes detrimental to performance in team sports when the demands of the activity, or other demands, subject the athlete to external and internal environmental stimuli of such intensity that his psycho-physical equilibrium deviates from its normal value. Because stress situations cannot be totally eliminated, athletes are taught how to deal with stress in a positive way by quickly recognizing any stress stimuli that are present and by dealing with these stimuli in a subjective manner. Dealing with stress requires psychological stability and the psychological capacity of the personality to bear stress.

Psychological stress experienced subjectively is caused by a very wide range of factors, factors which are the result of exogenous and endogenous stimuli and which may cause disruptions of considerable intensity. How athletes choose to cope with psychological stress depends on the intensity of the stimulus causing stress, on the internal conditions of the players' personalities, and on the subjective significance that is attached to these factors.

The disruptive potential of stress situations, and disruptive factors which result from the high and extremely diverse physical and psychological demands of team sports, are considerable. It is possible for psychological stress situations to arise when a player fails to solve correctly the diverse and various game tasks: when, for instance, a player quickly recognizes a game situation, and is able to analyze and to solve the problems arising out of it, but is unable to carry out the corresponding technical manoeuvres. The multiple reference system of teammates, opponents, referees, and spectators can also cause psychological stress. Problems in relationships among players such as group formation, limited acceptance, disputes, and lack of trust, tend to be detrimental to performance. Incomplete information about the opponent, causing an athlete to make an incorrect assessment and subsequently to overestimate the opponent's competitive strength and to underestimate his own may lead to psychological stress as well. According to statements of athletes, prejudice toward particular referees is often the cause of considerable stress before the game. Spectators are another potential source of psychological stress. Some players will find fans stressful (fear of making mistakes), while others experience stress with fans of theopposing team (catcalls, boos, etc.). Still other players will feel more at home in an atmosphere livened up by spectators and therefore tend to perform better. These examples show that players experience and cope with objective situations differently, and that no direct relationship or linear dependency can be established between potentially stressful situations and the psychological stress actually experienced. Psychological stress, therefore, is not caused by stressful situations, but by an individual's inability to cope with demands.

It has already been pointed out that situations which are not the direct result of training and competition can sometimes have an even more disruptive effect than those caused by the actual activity. These situations can range from personal worries at home, work, or university, to minor injuries, poor physical shape and poor organization, unfamiliar accomodations, restless nights, and fatigue from travelling. These and other situations, which have been identified over and over by players, often cause high levels of stress and can have a considerable effect on competitive performance. For this reason the number of such potential stress situations should be reduced to a minimum.

Psychological Ability of Players to Bear Stress

The psychological ability of players to bear stress is a complex personality feature determined by strength or weakness of their emotional factors, the structural relationships of basic personality traits, and by the attitudes of athletes. It enables players to fulfil highly varied demands made on them from both inside and outside athletic activity in a positive fashion and to cope with the stress situations caused by these demands. Coping with stress is a learning process in which steadily increasing psycho-physical demands are constantly tackled and positively dealt with by players. This means that although external conditions

116

remain the same, players can better meet the increased demands, making possible a reduction in stress and improved performance. Only when athletes gain the upper hand over these stress situations will a positive change in their overall regulatory systems occur and stimuli, which just a short while ago involved stress, represent only slight or very minimal disruptions in their athletic activity.

The psychological ability of players to bear stress is developed in immediate and concrete confrontation with potential stress conditions caused by objective demands, both in training and competition and outside the immediate athletic activity. During this process of conscious, active confrontation, the psychological ability to bear stress is developed within the athletes' general psychological resources.

This ability to bear stress, which is the goal of long-term education and athletic training, manifests itself in two forms: in psychological stability and in the capacity for coping with stress in a positive manner. We speak of the *psychological stability* of an athlete when great psycho-physical demands, whether from athletic activity or daily life, cause only minor modifications, or none at all, in his psychological structure. Players do not find the stimuli from their external and internal environment stressful, so their competitive ability remains steady.

Players can cope positively with psychological stress and perhaps completely overcome it by effecting a change in their psychological structure and by bringing additional functional systems into play. In this manner they are (a) able to compensate to the largest degree possible for the decrease in psychological performance caused by the presence of stress; (b) they are able to maintain performance ability; and (c) in some cases they are able to increase it.

An individual's entire psycho-physical system, which takes shape during the actual activity process, is involved in this process of coping with stress. In view of the complexity of team sports and the wide variety of demands which are made on players in different team sports, the ability of players to handle psychological stress is of particular importance. Great emotional demands are made on athletes in sports that require complex or acyclic motor sequences, and especially in team sports, where external conditions are constantly changing as a result of player interaction, direct and indirect opponent influence, ball movement, and the cheering or booing of individual actions by spectators. These factors often lead to psychological stress and can influence performance in competition. These considerations reinforce the notion that the greater the number of personality systems and system complexes involved in the execution of an action, the more competition results will depend on athletes' level of stress, on their psychological stability, and on their ability to handle stress in a positive manner.

The ability to bear stress depends, finally, on the state of development of the entire personality. The development of personality varies from individual to individual, even among players of the same team sport, since identical psychophysical demands do not lead to the development of the same personality traits in every case. Because of this, it would not be reasonable or prudent in physical education to attempt to produce a unified personality structure or to produce an individual with personality traits exactly in the degree and proportion desired. Each individual's ability to bear stress is governed by personality traits which are, in their nature, unevenly developed in some respects while being quite stable in others.

4. The Psychological Ability to Bear Stress During Education and Training in Team Sports

Increased psycho-physical demands in team sports, the objective result of the continual expansion of performance limits in sports, the decreasing gap in competitive performance among the best teams at the amateur and representative level, and fluctuations in performance among numerous teams make it imperative that more attention be given to the findings of psychological investigations of stress.

Fitness and coordination, as well as technique and tactics, are in most sports equally well-developed in athletes at the international level; thus, in title matches, psychological preparation, which includes the development of psychological stability and the capacity to cope with stress, is often the determining factor.

The development of the psychological ability to bear stress must therefore be given more attention than ever in the education and athletic training of athletes. We shall attempt to arrive at a few general conclusions for coaches and physical education teachers from the findings presented and from the empirical data obtained from our investigations into stress. The psychological ability to bear stress is developed only as the result of coping continually and successfully with various stress situations or factors that confront athletes in training and competition, as well as in other spheres of activity. Since the psychological ability to bear stress is not a simple psychological trait, but a very complex personality characteristic, it can be developed only during the process of general

The psychological ability to bear stress must be developed in a complex fashion and with purposeful organization during training and competition. The objective, therefore, cannot be the desire to eliminate completely all the elements that can cause psychological stress; this is impossible. Rather, it is more a systematic question of helping athletes to become accustomed to high psycho-physical demands in training and competition, so that stimuli originating from their external and internal environment are no longer stressful.

personality development. Every psychological trait, within its various structural relationships with other traits, influences an athlete's ability to bear stress, even if different valencies occur. This fact must be taken into consideration over the course of long-term education and athletic training of players.

The behaviour and performance of athletes are governed to a large extent by their guiding principles and motor drives. Among the guiding principles we find political and ideological convictions, interests, ideals, tendencies, and habits, as well as ensuing attitudes. These guiding principles are the personality qualities that determine the relation of athletes to their surroundings and to the concrete tasks which are required of them in training and competition. The development, consolidation, and implementation of these relationships must continually be influenced, as they have an effect on the quality and quantity of direct motor drives. Fundamental political and ideological convictions, a positive attitude toward sport and its demands, a high level of interest in the fulfilment of athletic objectives and goals, and positive ideals, tendencies, and attitudes are important foundations for the development of the psychological ability to bear stress and should be developed in a methodical and purposeful manner.

Motor drives are determined primarily by athletes' motives and needs; they play a direct role in triggering actions. The psychological stability of athletes and their ability to cope with psychological stress are determined by the content, markedness levels, strength, and effectiveness of these drives. Since athletes' motives in training and competition have a direct effect on their actions, great importance is given to their development, consolidation, and continual conscious implementation in education and athletic training. Social values are primarily the product of fundamental political and ideological convictions and of individual personality traits which interact closely with the habitual guiding principles and actual motor drives. The development of effective motives for competition within the process of training an athlete's psychological ability to bear stress is important, since these motives help determine to what extent an athletic objective will be fulfilled in the face of external and internal difficulties.

During the development of the athletes' personalities and of their psychological ability to bear stress, a prerequisite for and result of coming to terms with continually increasing psycho-physical demands, the ability to control one's actions and the entire process of motor regulation are very important. It is precisely in team sports, because of the diverse demands, that the way in which athletes have learned to direct their behaviour throughout daily life and athletic activity is a decisive factor. Particularly important in our investigation is the fact that athletes learn to control their behaviour successfully, especially in training and competition which require increased strength, unwavering self-control, and the ability to solve diverse and complex tasks independently and quickly. Since not all difficult situations and demands are subjectively considered difficult by individual players, they do not all require conscious guided actions. It can be observed during the development of this control ability that the same external demands and conditions (e.g., formidable opponents, spectators, unfavourable competitive conditions) and internal conflicts (e.g., negative psycho-physical state, high levels of anxiety and awareness of short-comings before competition) do not require the same skills of all players for the volitive control of their behaviour. Which skills are necessary for athletes to control their behaviour, and to cope successfully with external demands and conditions and internal conflicts, depends on the subjective retrospection of each player. The extent to which external demands and conditions and internal conflicts are experienced in different subjective manners can be demonstrated using this example of an empirical investigation of soccer players. In this study, the significance of an important championship or critical regulation game is experienced by 35% of the players as being conducive to performance, by 40% of the players as causing no particular excitement, and by 25% of the players as hindering their performance because of negative attitudes toward the game and lack of self-confidence. The superiority of opponents is experienced by 20% of the players as being beneficial, by 40% as being neither beneficial nor detrimental, and by 40% of the players as being detrimental.

From this investigation coaches and physical education teachers can see that to make a practical assessment of the skills that already exist or of those that have yet to be developed, they need facts that have been scientifically verified concerning the subjective experience of players, the external demands that are routinely made upon them, and the external conflicts they must face. Only then will they be able to influence, on an individual basis, the development of skills that effect the conscious control of behaviour and attitudes.

The psychological ability to bear stress must be developed in a complex fashion and with purposeful organization during training and competition. The objective, therefore, cannot be the desire to eliminate completely all the elements that can cause psychological stress; this is impossible. Rather, it is more a systematic question of helping athletes to become accustomed to high psycho-physical demands in training and competition, so that stimuli originating from their external and internal environment are no longer stressful. Since psychological stress may still appear, even in the cases of the best general psychological preparation, the ability of players to cope successfully with situations involving psychological stress must be developed and consolidated during athletic activity along with all other psychological traits, especially specific competitive traits. Athletes must change their psychological structure without decreasing performance. The capacity for dealing with stress, like any other ability, develops only with practice. Feelings of success stemming from psychological stress situations that have been coped with successfully are conducive to this process.

Training and competition, like any other athletic activity, are aimed at adapting the entire psycho-physical systems of athletes' to continually increasing demands and at increasing athletes' ability to handle stress at continually higher levels. The goal of these investigations has been to assess the individual levels of stress, and the effect of stress-causing stimuli under concrete sports-specific situations, in order to draw conclusions concerning the psychological ability to bear stress as a complex, habitual personality characteristic among individual players. Results reached by sports psychologists utilizing various methods has enabled coaches to work individually with each athlete.

A determination of psychological stress and psychological ability to bear stress is possible with an analysis of the outcome of the activity, the completion of the activity, actual psychological states, and changes in psychological functional sequences. Each of these can be used by coaches and exercise instructors as a basis for their individual educational activities.

Stress factors whose origins do not lie in sports, but which influence athletic performance, are to be avoided or reduced as much as possible by means of working individually with each athlete. Coaches can prevent social problems in relationships among players by training the group in a purposeful manner. Problems with work or at school can be prevented by working closely with those in charge. The inclusion of parents or spouses in the formation of athletic objectives can help prevent family problems. Finally, athletes must learn to cope with all these situations in a positive manner and in such a way that performance in competition is not affected.

CHAPTER 9

The Significance of Personal and Social Factors for Competitive Performance in Soccer

1. Theoretical Formulation and Methodology of the Investigations

Internal and External Conditions in Personality Development

Athletes must deal with a number of situations in practice and in competition in order to perform up to their full potential. Many of these can be overcome by the inner capacities of the personality. Every personality, however, is characterized by its own specific structure of general, specific, and individual traits; thus identical external conditions will produce different responses in different athletes.

Whenever an individual's psychological state and mental and emotional systems succeed in overcoming an external condition, a specific psychological response is created. Each psychological process occurs within the framework of a specific psychological state, a state which governs an individual's actions and causes his/her changes (9:206). During this psychological process, an interaction occurs between the external condition and the inner state of the personality. External or environmental conditions determine athletes' actions and influence their behaviour. Athletes confront and assimilate these conditions, thus creating internal conditions. During the course of further activity, these conditions, internalized and reinforced, find their expression in the athlete's behaviour. Specific conditions trigger behaviour, which is controlled by the personality. Behaviour is no longer shaped exclusively by the present situation, but also by the athlete's personality. In response to the "dialectical conflict" between internal and external conditions, according to Hiebsch and Vorwerg, (3) external conditions become the primary factors governing athletes' behaviour. This opinion, however, seems to contradict the fact that external conditions always clash with internal determining conditions.

Since athletes' performance is subject to this interaction between internal and external conditions, it is important to investigate the inner psychological laws that govern the effect of external influence. It is hypothesized here that the negative effect of external influence decreases as internal reference systems of the personality become more stable.

The Significance of Social Relationships in Team Sports

The social elements of action and behaviour serve as a fundamental point of reference in the dialectical interaction between internal and external conditions and, subsequently, in performance. It is hypothesized that since athletes are required to achieve a collective result, social factors heavily influence a player's performance. The social relationship in team sports is critically important to the success of the team, since the actions of individual players can affect the entire team. On the other hand, team achievements establish norms which act as incentives for individual players to continually improve their performance. We support the view of Bachmann, who says: "Human behaviour is activated and determined by the group's attitude toward achievement and by the dynamic interaction between demands, performance, and collective evaluation from which it then receives its impulses and orientation" (1:559).

The development of collective personality has become the goal in individual development. Boshowitsch stresses: "...the psychological development, is social by nature and develops under the decisive influence of the social environment (2:93)."

It is hypothesized, on this basis, that the most important conditions for personality development are athletes' social relationships and activities. Educators in the German Democratic Republic regard collective education not merely as one of several methods but as the basis for the development of socialistic personalities. We further hypothesize that the social structure of teams establishes individual norms for behaviour and achievement. These, in turn, form the fundamental components for psychological stability or lability. This relationship must not be seen as one-sided, since an athlete's personality, in turn, influences the structure and characteristics of the social group to which the athlete belongs. This interdependent relationship, and the socio-psychological and socio-pedagogical activity which follows from it and which shapes the entire personality, contributes to the differentiation, personal image, and quantitative expansion of the performance potential of the athlete's personality. The end result is the harmonious and all-round development of the athlete.

This interdependence within the team exists primarily at the athlete/athlete, athlete/team, athlete/coach, team/coach/officials levels, and is realized through cooperation. Cooperation improves achievement by increasing individual productive forces; this in turn gives rise to greater competitive enthusiasm and the establishment of a new collective and productive force.

Athletic training and competition is social by nature. Social cooperation can positively influence athletic ability either directly, by improving team performance as a result of better cooperation, or indirectly, by encouraging individual competitive ability through team spirit. This cooperation effect can have two outcomes. On the one hand, as a result of the influence of the group on the willingness to achieve, the competitive ability of individual players is improved; on the other hand, as a result of cooperation, the competitive ability of the team is increased. The team's achievements during this process are always greater than the total sum of the players' individual achievements.

Conflicts can be detrimental to the team if they are not candidly discussed and resolved. This is particularly true in team sports where cooperation is essential to successful competition. Not only do conflicts hinder teamwork, they also hinder a player's individual technical and tactical actions. In competition it is highly likely that conflicts detract from the results to be obtained through cooperation and subsequently from the results themselves.

It goes without saying that coaches and managers must try to create an advantage for their own team by establishing good interpersonal relationships. They must guide the development of the group in such a way that the attitudes of individual players are directed toward fulfilling collective and individual objectives. The behaviour of any one athlete toward his goals, his teammates, his coach, and his opponents is vital important to his own performance and to the outcome of the game. Athletes must learn to subordinate their personal interests to those of the team. Competitive ability and performance in individual players grows as a result of a willingness to exert themselves and to cooperate actively in the realization of the team's goals.

The athlete's social relationships outside of competition are important as well. There is an inseparable link, sometimes even a direct relationship, between athletic activity and extra-curricular activity. The athlete's personal life can be the immediate cause of difficulties in athletic performance. The reverse, of course, is also possible; athletic activities can influence the individual athlete's private sphere.

In summary, in seeking to maximize the competitive ability of an athlete, the objective is to improve performance by building the athlete's willingness to exert himself or herself. This willingness and the individual strength potential it fosters can be increased only if the athlete is willing to cooperate actively in the realization of team goals.

Conflicts exist between behavioural demands and the the athlete's personal state. According to what is, perhaps, the most fundamental law of Marxist dialectics, inner conflicts are the driving force behind growth. When this law is applied to personality growth, the implication is a correlation between the actual personal state and higher performance. The development of behavioural traits generally occurs in collective interaction. The group in which athletes realize their basic performance relationships constitutes a fundamental condition for development.

According to Kossakowski (6), norms and social relationships within the basic group are particularly important in determining the attitudes and behavioural traits of the individual.

The Significance of Personal Factors in Performance Development

Athletes are continually confronted with demands in training and competition, as well as in activities outside of sports, that influence athletic ability. Players must meet the performance demands which are made on them in competition. For this reason, it is especially important to analyze the effects of these demands on the subjective response of players.

The way in which athletes deal with various stimuli depends largely on the developmental levels of their personalities. This is especially true when players have to cope with objective and situative conditions in competition. How intensely these factors are experienced, and whether they have a positive or negative influence on performance (or no effect at all), depends on the athletes' subjective and individual states.

A distinction is made between the two types of psychological ability to bear stress, psychological weakness, and psychological stability. Psychologically stable athletes are less susceptible to stress-causing stimuli than psychologically weak athletes. In psychologically weak athletes, specific stimuli trigger significant psychological stress reactions; these, however, can be dealt with. Certain psychological traits can be developed to an extent that the athletes' performance remains constant, or even improves. In order to overcome stress, we must determine which conditions affect performance and how athletes can deal with these conditions. Inter-individual and intra-individual differences are, alike, factors in the psychological resilience of athletes.

In order to influence the development of personality traits in athletes, an understanding of their inner characteristics is necessary. It is believed that the psychological traits of athletes are both a prerequisite for and a result of their activities. The development of these traits is sport and training specific, with social relationships playing a fundamental role.

Research Methodology

Athletes' personality characteristics and social variables may be determined by several methods. It is hypothesized that there are objective demands in the activity of athletes that must be dealt with. Specific responses to these demands are the result. As players develop, a solid relationship structure forms which enables them to guide themselves and to reflect the effect of external influences. Athletes are both subject and object during the course of their activity, as they are affected by, and affect, changes to their environment. This reinforces the fact that team players must be able to exercise self-control in order to influence their behaviour. Self-observation and self-discipline are indispensable prerequisites for this purpose. Team players are therefore better able to observe and to judge the course of their physical and psychological processes, and to compare these processes with the outcome of their activity by reference to their experiences and to the comparisons that can be made between various performance requirements.

Traditional paper and pencil tests and questionnaires are used for these assessments to provide information about the subjective way in which players experience personal and social factors. The tests include:

1. Questionnaires for studying the effect of progressive game conditions, the aim of which is to record situations relevant to athletes in competition and the effects of social relationships with coaches, teammates, opponents, and spectators, as well as the effect of individual factors such as techniques, tactics and physical condition.
2. Questionnaires for studying the effect of general performance conditions;
3. Questionnaires for self-evaluation, and for the evaluation of others for personality traits which determine collective behaviour, mental disposition towards performance, guiding traits, and individual behaviour (the result of attitudes toward oneself).
4. Group evaluation procedures with questions on interpersonal relationships (e.g., in leisure time) and on various performance and behavioural characteristics (e.g., in competition and practice).

The above test battery was used three times within the space of two and one half years.

Table 28 Game situations which players experienced as being the most detrimental to performance.

	$\bar{x}$		
	Test 1	Test 2	Test 3
1. During the game I was continually criticized from the coach's bench.	3.80	3.91	3.87
2. I was unable to complete several tactical actions.	3.75	3.83	3.70
3. I was unable to complete some actions. As a result, I was harrassed by a few teammates.	3.75	3.78	3.65
4. Right at the beginning of the game I was unsucessful in taking the ball, which is normally no problem for me. This makes our game uncertain.	3.70	4.00	3.78
5. During the course of the game considerable shortcomings in my physical fitness became apparent.	3.70	3.74	3.70
6. Because my passes quite often do not reach the teammates I intend, promising attacking plays are interrupted.	3.65	3.78	3.70

2. Markedness Levels of Specific Progressive Game and General Performance Conditions, Psychological Characteristics and Social Relationships

Individual Responses to Specific Game Flow

The course of a game is characterized by constantly changing situations which athletes experience actively, that, is in the process of playing the game. Athletes experience a continuous chain of individual and collective feelings—feelings of

Table 29 Game situations which players experienced as being the most conducive to performance.

	$\bar{x}$		
	Test 1	Test 2	Test 3
1. I am often successful at outplaying my opponents and at blocking goals.	1.45	1.52	1.57
2. Spectators especially encourage me personally in this home game.	1.45	1.61	1.70
3. It turns out that I am superior to my opponent in every respect.	1.45	1.91	1.70
4. We were two goals behind. After a subsequent goal our performance improved considerably.	1.55	1.73	1.78
5. I made several good passes, which initiated goal-blocking attacks.	1.65	1.96	1.91

success and of failure—which then have either a positive or negative effect on performance. In our research it was apparent that personal and social relationships shape behaviour and determine performance to a considerable extent. Situations which athletes experienced as being the most detrimental to performance are presented in Table 28. Situations which athletes experienced as being most favourable to performance are shown in Table 29.

Personal factors caused the strongest psychological stress reactions among players and were highly significant in training and preparation for competition.

Unsuccessful movements and plays (actions related to player's techniques) have a particularly negative effect on performance; whereas successful techniques have the most positive effect on players (see Table 30). The highly negative effect of technique on players is also expressed in the difference (d) values between positive and negative situations. They constitute the greatest differences among all d values. Since some relatively high d values are also found for tactics, and for physical and fitness factors, the personal factors seem

Table 30   Personal related factors and their effects on athletes.

Personal Factors	Situations		
	Positive $\overline{x}_1$	Negative $\overline{x}_2$	Difference $d = \overline{x}_2 - \overline{x}_1$
Physical fitness factors			
Test 1	1.98	3.43	1.45
Test 2	2.11	3.55	1.44
Test 3	1.97	3.46	1.49
Technical actions			
Test 1	1.85	3.65	1.80
Test 2	1.86	3.90	2.04
Test 3	1.84	3.66	1.82
Tactical actions			
Test 1	1.93	3.50	1.57
Test 2	2.10	3.75	1.65
Test 3	1.97	3.58	1.61

to be the most significant domain for athletes. Furthermore, for all three factors in this area, no significant differences in means were found across the three testings. Thus, it would appear that the influence of positive and negative situations has an almost constant and significant influence on athletes.

In respect to social factors (Table 31), positive spectator response has the most positive effect on performance. Negative situations with teammates, such as unjust criticism or misunderstandings, have the most detrimental effect. The situations which are related to the opponent do not elicit either strong positive or negative responses, as is the case in the other three areas. Athletes, it would appear, do not experience collective opponents to be particularly conducive or detrimental to their performance. The following situation, however, has a different effect: "It turns out that I am superior to my opponent in every respect," is experienced by all players as being conducive or detrimental to performance and affect the psychological preparation of individual players for their tasks within the framework of collective game preparation.

Table 31   Social related factors and their effects on athletes.

Social Factors	Situations		
	Positive $\bar{x}_1$	Negative $\bar{x}_2$	Difference $d = \bar{x}_2 - \bar{x}_1$
Relationship with coach			
Test 1	1.92	3.45	1.53
Test 2	2.11	3.46	1.35
Test 3	2.00	3.43	1.43
Relationship with own team			
Test 1	1.83	3.58	1.75
Test 2	2.40	3.65	1.25
Test 3	1.96	3.42	1.46
Relationship with opponent			
Test 1	2.07	3.08	1.01
Test 2	2.16	3.20	1.04
Test 3	2.19	3.22	1.03
Relationship with spectators			
Test 1	1.58	3.30	1.72
Test 2	1.85	3.51	1.66
Test 3	1.87	3.38	1.51

The relationships experienced between personal and social factors of specific progressive game conditions highlight the uniformity of these areas in training and education.

In each investigation (Test 1 through Test 3), highly substantiated relationships between the social and personal domains appear. Both these areas seem to be inextricably linked in the experiences of players. The relationships between the most important factors in these areas were examined in the hope that a more exact understanding might be achieved. The most significant relationships were those to be found between "criticism from coaches" and "unsuccessful tactics." and between "negative situations with teammates" and "unsuccessful tactics."

Table 32   Performance conditions which players experienced as being the
most detrimental to performance.

	$\bar{x}$		
	Test 1	Test 2	Test 3
1. Feeling of extremely poor physical shape.	3.55	3.65	3.65
2. Before the game I had great feelings of failure outside of sports.	3.50	3.57	3.61
3. I am in an extremely bad mood.	3.45	3.43	3.39
4. I feel uneasy going into the game because during the last game spectators were very critical of me.	3.25	3.70	3.57
5. Spectators have a particularly negative attitude towards their own team.	3.45	3.61	3.30
6. In single combat situation against my immediate opponent I was often inferior.	3.25	3.48	3.26

Definite relationships may also be found between the situations represented by "criticism from coaches" and "unsuccessful technique", and between "unsuccessful technique and tactics."

In the first investigation a relationship was also observed between "negative situations with teammates" and "unsuccessful technique." In the later investigations, the relationship is not as close; neither criteria continue to be experienced in this uniform manner. In the first and second studies no relationships were found to exist between "negative experiences/situations with opponents" and "unsuccessful technical/tactical actions". This changes, however, in the third investigation, where the relationship is observed to be much closer. Players associate strongly with both areas in their experience, and the value between "negative experiences with opponents" and "unsuccessful tactical/actions" is highly significant.

Table 33   Performance conditions which players experienced as being the most conducive to performance.

	$\bar{x}$		
	Test 1	Test 2	Test 3
1. Spectators have a particularly positive attitude towards their own team.	1.40	1.57	1.48
2. Home game before a large crowd.	1.60	1.57	1.52
3. I feel at ease going into the game, as spectators applauded me quite alot during the last game.	1.65	1.70	1.83
4. Feeling of the best physical shape.	1.70	1.65	1.57
5. Coach really praised me for my results in the last game.	1.70	1.91	1.83
6. I am in a mood where I could "take the world".	1.85	1.78	1.74

How Players Experience General Performance Conditions

Similar to the above, the performance conditions which athletes experience as being the most detrimental and conducive to performance are summarized in Tables 32 and 33.

Results concerning the stimulating or stressful effect of athletes' personal factors (Table 34) show that physical fitness and emotional factors have the greatest influence on players. It is also in this area that we find the greatest differences between positive and negative responses. The athletes' high level of physical fitness is the most reassuring variable among all of the personal factors. Emotional states have a similar positive effect; especially that of putting the team and its individual players in a positive frame of mind. On the other hand, poor physical fitness is experienced by athletes most negatively. These conclusions reveal how close the relationship is between successful methodical training (which among other things develops fitness to high levels) and its positive

Table 34   Effect of athlete's personal related factors.

Personal Factors	Conditions		
	Positive $\bar{x}_1$	Negative $\bar{x}_2$	Difference $d = \bar{x}_2 - \bar{x}_1$
Physical shape			
Test 1	2.06	3.33	1.27
Test 2	1.80	3.45	1.65
Test 3	1.74	3.39	1.65
Feelings of success/failure			
Test 1	1.98	3.38	1.40
Test 2	1.94	3.04	1.10
Test 3	1.96	3.10	1.14
Feelings of certainty/uncertainty			
Test 1	2.23	2.97	0.74
Test 2	2.22	2.94	0.72
Test 3	2.29	2.87	0.58
Emotional states			
Test 1	2.05	3.22	1.17
Test 2	1.98	3.47	1.49
Test 3	1.84	3.22	1.38

psychological effect.

Table 35 presents the effect of social factors on athletes.

The results also underscore the fact that positive spectator reactions have a highly stimulating effect on players, whereas, for the most part, critical reactions only become important to players in subsequent games.

The effects of spectator reaction on an athlete's performance might account, therefore, for the discrepancy which is often found between away and home games. Thus, preparing for the reactions of spectators should make up an important part of psychological preparation. Players must be convinced that spectators cannot exert a direct influence on their performance. They must

Table 35   Effect of athletes' social related factors.

Social Factors	Conditions		
	Positive	Negative	Difference
	$\bar{x}_1$	$\bar{x}_2$	$d = \bar{x}_2 - \bar{x}_1$
Relationship with opponent			
Test 1	2.07	3.11	1.04
Test 2	1.97	3.44	1.47
Test 3	2.17	3.19	1.02
Relationship with spectators			
Test 1	1.55	2.97	1.42
Test 2	1.55	3.31	1.78
Test 3	1.61	3.22	1.61

realize that spectators only indirectly affect their performance by affecting their psychological states. Over the course of long-term preparation, mental toughness must be developed; the aim is to improve motor and behaviour control, as it is motor and behaviour control that is chiefly responsible for the establishment of an inner equilibrium in psychologically stressful situation. The special role played by these and other related factors in overcoming demands in team sports will be discussed in the next section. The influence of opponents on the players is given a relatively low classification. There is a little difference in the assessment of stress caused by opponents or by spectators, but considerable difference exists in the stimulation they provoke.

Personality Profile Analysis

In all previous sports-psychology investigations concerning personality of athletes, two basic trends in personality determination, and in its particular sports-specific and individual characteristics, may be observed: (a) the presentation of the personality profile or athlete's psychogramme and (b) the factor-analytically determined structural relationships and areas of personality.

The profile presentation indicates the characteristic levels of individual traits and makes possible an analysis of trends in development. The disadvan-

Table 36   Factor I - collective behaviour.

Ranking	Item Loading	Description of Items/ Characteristic Behaviour	No.*
1	.819	social and moral behaviour	16
2	.765	collective spirit	20
3	.742	reliability	5
4	.703	civic and patriotic bebaviour	17
5	.616	independence	7
6	.597	sociability	15
7	.595	self-control	21
8	.501	determination	1

* Corresponds to the sequence of the description of the traits.

Table 37   Factor II - mental performance.

Ranking	Item Loading	Description of Items/ Characteristic Behaviour	No.
1	.814	ability to distribute attention	27
2	.791	ability to make combinations	19
3	.789	ability to take in the entire game	11
4	.694	ability to switch attention	28
5	.670	agility of thought processes	12
6	.666	anticipation ability	10
7	.592	powers of observation and judgement	2

tage of this approach, however, is that it does not provide any information about the structural relationships that hold between the personality traits. The nature of these structural relationships can be determined using factor analysis. The factor analytic approach provides groupings of personality dispositions according to uniform characteristics.

It is very important that several approaches be used in personality analysis. More than one approach will provide a better understanding of personality structure, developmental characteristics, and the strength of individual charac-

Table 38   Factor III – mental toughness/will-power.

Ranking	Item Loading	Description of Items/ Characteristic Behaviour	No.
1	.803	will-power	4
2	.736	ability to improve performance	9
3	.631	willingness to take risks	8
4	.613	vigourness of will	23
5	.567	determination	1
6	.514	adaptability	6
7	.511	resolution	18
8	.505	psychological resilience	22

Table 39   Factor IV – attitude toward oneself.

Ranking	Item Loading	Description of Items/ Characteristic Behaviour	No.
1	.715	need for admiration	14
2	.672	desire to experience	26
3	.537	self-confidence	3
4	.501	ability to accomplish	25
5	.437	self-esteem	13

teristics. Furthermore, it will compensate for variations in the levels of individual characteristics, variations that can cause changes in the structural relationships of the personality traits.

In the following section, an attempt is made to determine the role of major or minor personality qualities in the overall structure of personality. Factor analysis is used for this purpose. Krause and Lander (7) portray the procedure as a method of analysing relationships between random and interdependent personality characteristics by attributing these characteristics to specific common complexes of causes, the factors. Their objective is to analyse a large number of variables in order to understand a smaller number of factors that have personality characteristics related to team sports. These factors, shown in Tables 36 to 39, are:

Factor I   – collective behaviour;
Factor II – mental performance;
Factor III – mental toughness (will power); and
Factor IV – attitude toward oneself.

Items which demonstrate the highest item-loading within an individual factor are observed to be the most important determinants of that factor. On the basis of this research, it was deemed necessary that specific, continuous, and careful attention be given to the development of these factors.

Social Relationships Within the Team

It is assumed that social relationships within the team have a profound influence on the psychological states of players, and, hence, on their playing performance.

Social relationships influence both the group and the individual players of which the group consists. Some of these relationships were examined using players who were observed to cooperate with each other in training and competition. The objective of the investigation was to discover how individual players make decisions in various demanding situations and, further, to investigate the dynamics of the team in order to find ways of controlling its development. For this purpose, the GAP (Group Analysis Procedure) was used in all three tests. The GAP described in Chapter 5 presents four categories of questions related to (1) competition, (2) leisure, (3) political activities discussion, and (4) training intensity. A fifth category was added. This category referred to leadership role/independent training in small groups. Various aspects of relationships were studied. Correlation coefficients between the individual GAP categories were calculated (Table 40) in order to work out the structure of the social aspects of relationships.

All correlations except one are significant, with 75% of the values significant at the .01 level. It is observed that in general, the highest correlations are associated with performance. This suggests that how a player performs and how he is regarded by his teammates are a common characteristic of social collectivity. The performance of an athlete is therefore a factor of considerable importance in his ranking within the group and the actual performance capability of an athlete, a main point of reference for players in the assessment of their relationships with each other. The performance factor is given a significantly more positive assessment.

Overall, the results of this investigation support Karpinski's (5) prerequisites for a good sports team. They include frequent positive relationships within

Table 40   Relationship (r) among the five GAP categories.

Question	Test 1 n = 21	Test 2 n = 23	Test 3 n = 23
1-3	0.46	0.45	0.27
1-2	0.76	0.85	0.69
1-4	0.79	0.77	0.58
1-5	0.79	0.84	0.72
2-3	0.49	0.54	0.43
2-4	0.65	0.78	0.53
2-5	0.73	0.82	0.76
3-4	0.76	0.75	0.69
3-5	0.73	0.72	0.68
4-5	0.89	0.94	0.78

the group, minimal outside relationships, low team turnover, a high number of frequently chosen athletes, and a high level of athletic activity. It was observed, however, that the athletic ability of individual players was the prime consideration and that important attitudes and characteristics were not of major concern.

Another important hypothesis of the study is that the relationship between the group and the individual is a dialectic one, for the social determination of the human personality takes place in behaviour that occurs in a tangible social group, and is subject to its conditions (3). The group of athletes, with its norms and its structure, also determines the behaviour and attitudes of its members.

In the evaluations of the attitudes of members in the group, behaviour is judged according to specific norms and according to the fulfillment of specific demands. The degree to which the norms and demands are met depends to a large extent upon the nature of the team and upon the athletes' personal characteristics.

The inner system of the personality and social integration determine the extent to which external conditions will have an effect. Athletes with strong, marked personality traits and corresponding social behaviour will cope with these conditions better than those whose personality traits and social position are weak. Those athletes with marked personality traits are sociable, and integrate well in their groups. "The more marked the structure of the inner condition of the social group of individual players, the more group-specific or individually differentiated and reinforced it is, and the more it acts as a special type of filter to assimilate social norms and values and to select, absorb, reject, or gradually transform external influences in its own way (8:19)."

Strong influences from external factors may bring about strong fluctuations in players' competitive and training performance. A group which is well developed can compensate for negative competitive conditions, to a certain extent, just as a team with a low level of development will experience stress situations to a considerably greater degree during performance.

A number of correlations between the athletes' personal characteristics (intellectual/mental characteristics, collective behaviour,and mental toughness) and their social status within the group were examined. But, no consistent statistically significant relationships were found.

3. Implications for Coaching

The collective and individual aspects are dealt with separately in this section: the purpose is to draw attention to those components of the coaching process that are distinct. Needless to say, the philosophy of collective development remains the determining factor in the coaching process; and the individual and social aspects of coaching, although separable in theory, are not, according to the East German approach, separable in practice.

Team Development

The development of collectives requires determined and methodical work. Sports officials must have a thorough knowledge of the developmental level of the team, of its tasks, and of the prevailing norms and social relationships that exist among its members. It must be ensured:

- That the team is able to solve its political and ideological training tasks with respect to its class;
- That group norms and objectives correspond with those of society, as much as possible, in order to make coaching highly effective;
- That the role of each individual player is clear and that the goal is to improve one's position in the group; and
- That management, by means of concrete demands, evaluation, and correction, continually influences the performance and behaviour of the team.

The completion of an athletic activity is always governed and influenced by social processes. With each other and for each other, the motto of socialist society shapes the individuality of the personality. The formation of strong enthusiastic groups is the basic form and principle means for educating and forming socialist personalities.

The research has shown that the contents and structure of social judgements are influenced decisively by athletic performance. The typical characteristic of socialist groups is, however, the unity between performance and behaviour. Furthermore, the investigation determined a high consistency in response to the individual questions in GAP, for social structure. The high number of positive attitudes is proof that specific demands made in a group have been fulfilled. Slight variability, caused mainly by athletic activity, can have a negative effect on the team's performance if the leading players do not show proof of suitable development levels in their personalities. As the investigation shows, leading athletes do not always conform to the required personality characteristics. During periods of stress in competition, the absence of individual intrapersonal prerequisites can be compensated for, to a certain extent, by the team. However, a team that must compensate in this way will reach its performance limits sooner. Successful cooperation on a team presupposes the presence of adequate psychological performance prerequisites (abilities, behavioural traits, skills) for solving the tasks that have been set. The leading player on the team must possess these prerequisites (8).

The management of a team, therefore, must aim at improving the team through concrete measures in order to improve the prerequisites of the athletes' personalities. Behavioural demands that effect changes in attitudes and psychological traits should be made by the team on its leading players. Athletes demonstrate the appropriate behaviour if their goal is to fulfil the demands which are expected of them. This affects the leading players as well as the younger lesser skilled players of the group. Those responsible for the education of athletes should improve the developmental levels of athletes through concrete demands. They must establish norms which are in keeping with the levels of the team, which prompt motivation, and which form objectives and guiding standards for the entire team.

The investigations of the social structure and markedness levels of personality traits in the collective sphere has two important implications: (1) Team norms must be established which focus on general and specific goals. These norms have a great influence on athletic performance. They include norms which result from demands made in competition, norms which affect the organization of intensive training, and norms for leisure time behaviour. (2) There must be an increase in the variability of the team, in order that those athletes with the best behaviour and attitudes assume a befitting social position.

Coaches will utilize those athletes who are best integrated into the social group. Since attitudes and behaviour outside of competition as well as performance during competition influence social position, the following methods for distribution of tasks should be used:

1. There must be a purposeful distribution of tasks to suitable athletes in the different areas of activity (political/ideological sphere, preparation for competition and game organization, practice, and leisure time).

2. Concrete demands with a limited content must be fulfilled by the team over a long period of time.

3. An evaluation of task fulfillment by each team member must be conducted.

4. Principles of collective behaviour must be stressed in the training programmes.

Evaluations should take place at specific time intervals during the athletic season. They should give coaches an overall view of the development levels of social performance. Actual behaviour can be assessed using concrete measures from which additional pedagogical measures may be derived for the educational process.

Individual Development

In order for athletes to develop socialist personalities, the following two education aims must be fulfilled:

1. Basic ideological principles and their resulting attitudes towards the concrete demands in training and competition must be developed and reinforced.

2. Psychological traits, which, as moral qualities, characterize the actions and behaviour of athletes in all demanding areas of their social lives and which, as psychological competitive traits, constitute the specific performance prerequisites in competition, must be developed and reinforced.

Factor analysis demonstrates that one's attitude toward oneself is developed to a greater extent than one's attitude towards the group. For this reason, characteristics such as the need for admiration, the need for new experiences, and the need for self-esteem, should be used for the development of collective behaviour. This can be accomplished by making athletes even more aware of the collective framework of individual behaviour. The main emphasis in education lies in social contact, collective spirit, and social and moral behaviour.

Strong and competitively stable athletes are distinguished by strong attitudes and mental toughness. The above mentioned research results emphasize the need for coaches to place characteristics such as determination, adaptive ability, and willpower in the centre of the coaching process. Coaches should teach players to:

1. Think decisions through quickly and carefully and to translate them into action in situations where external resistance is offered.

2. Adapt to difficulties (handicap situations, bad weather, etc.) under adverse conditions.

3. Develop willpower in suitable training and competition situations.

4. Pursue their goals with the same willpower, doggedness, persistence, and ambition, even when difficulties arise, and while pushing themselves to the limit.

This specific aspect of mental toughness can, and must, take priority in athletic development during training and competition in accordance with the characteristics listed in methodical organization and in preparation for competition. Attention should be drawn to the fact that guiding traits become effective only with a solid base of self-confidence. It is seldom possible to compensate for low levels of self-confidence with well-developed mental toughness alone.

In the area of mental characteristics needed in competition, distributive attention, game creativity, overview of the game, ability to switch attention, and focused attention are the most important. For this reason, they should become the focal point in continued work with athletes. These results indicate that athletes should be taught to:

- understand and solve complicated situations quickly and be able to use them for their own benefit;
- act in a collected manner and keep an overview of the game in critical situations;
- keep their attention on several players or actions; and
- switch their attention from observing a game manoeuvre into high level participation in the action.

The presence of intellectual/mental characteristics during the course of the game corroborates greatly with this investigation. It is therefore important that educational processes create relevant and educational demands which challenge and stimulate athletes according to their abilities in sports as well as in other activities outside sports.

Only when athletes use all of the methodological and psychological training methods at their disposal will they be up to the mental demands which are made on their personalities during creative participation. Where personality structure is concerned, highly developed intellectual capacity cannot be a substitute for poorly developed mental toughness or for lack of self-confidence.

Psychological Considerations in Immediate Game Preparation

In view of the different ways in which stress-causing stimuli are experienced, general game flow and athletes' general performance must be examined. Competition requires athletes to exert themselves to the limits of their subjective performance ability. Without sufficient preparation, the athlete would not be able to meet competition requirements. Therefore, in training, athletes must prepare in such a way that they achieve the highest possible results in competition, taking into consideration their particular individual capacities.

Factors causing the greatest individual stress in competition are unsuccessful technical actions, unsuccessful tactical actions, and poor physical conditions.

In the social sphere, tension or a feeling of failure (the result of relationships with individual players) place the greatest demands on the athletes psychological stability. Other factors resulting in stress are unfair criticism by teammates, misunderstandings in the game, continual criticism by coach during the game, and inferior position to direct opponent. These negative situations can be explained by low development levels of collective behaviour, mental toughness, and specific mental characteristics of the game. It is necessary to compensate for these in order to reduce the negative effect on performance of additional stressors.

Conditions which influence athletes before competition can also have a considerable effect during competition. The highly corroborated relationships between the personal and social sphere point out that even before performance demands have begun, these areas can have a decisive effect on eagerness to perform. Extensive attention should be given to personal and social relationships before competition in view of their significance in competition.

On the basis of our research, the following aspects must be considered:

1. High fitness level has a stimulatory effect for all athletes. It greatly influences psychological stability and is an important criterion in game preparation and in unifying the team.

2. An optimistic mood should be created for each individual before competition.

3. Attitudes towards spectators are important to athletes. They should always understand that negative spectator response has no direct influence on the game; only their performance can determine the game outcome.

4. Particular features of opponents' performance should be collectively analysed by the team and, in special cases, by individual players. This will create an actual performance expectation.

Enabling athletes to approach situations successfully and to develop psychological stability in the face of specific competitive demands can make a considerable contribution to stabilizing athletes' self-confidence. This should be reinforced before competition so that athletes are prepared to successfully deal with specific demands made during the course of play.

Chapter 10

Application of Psycho-Regulatory Techniques in Team Sports

1. Introduction

Significance of Psycho-Regulatory Techniques in Sports

Progress in athletic performance is achieved primarily by increasing the quantity and quality of the demands made on athletes. When the athletes have learned all the technical elements of a sport (i.e., skill), training intensification becomes the decisive and dynamic factor in performance development. Sports psychology is therefore used to tap performance reserves. Psycho-regulatory techniques (PRT) have been implemented in training to an increasing extent over the last few years. The main objective of these techniques is to achieve the relaxation and complete mobilization of an athlete's resources. This includes the following:

- Improving functional fitness while preventing excessive fatigue and accelerating recovery;
- Improving technical motor sequences through proper mental imagery and of the execution of movements;
- Improving technical preparation with activity programmes for different variations in competitive situations; and
- Improving the athlete's psychological states through positive emotional influences.

Sports psychology offers a range of different PRTs which help athletes to control their psychological states. The success of these procedures largely depends on the athlete's familiarity with the procedures, and the extent to which he or she makes use of them.

Psychological Foundations for Psycho-Regulatory Techniques

Psycho-Regulatory Techniques are based on the close relationship which exists between functions of the higher brain centres in the central nervous system (thought, linguistic, and imagination processes), on the one hand, and bodily autonomic functions and ideomotor reactions, on the other.

The activity of muscles and internal organs, indeed of the entire organism, is controlled and regulated by the nervous system, with the brain functioning as the command centre. Functioning as the command centre, the brain keeps the individual functions in tune with each other and brings them into line with changing conditions. Psychological processes (perception, emotions, and thought) take place in the brain, and are connected psycho-physically with specific bodily processes. These fundamental nervous connections develop and are consolidated throughout the life of the individual, through experience and learning. It follows that psychological influencing of the organism can be learned.

The functions of the internal organs, the heart, circulatory system, digestive system, etc., can sometimes be psychogenically influenced by high levels of excitement, such as those which are present before an important competition. Since these functions are controlled by the involuntary (autonomic) nervous system, they are more difficult to influence than voluntary movements. Nevertheless, they are open to psychological regulation. This regulation can be brought about by the use of vivid mental conceptions, conceptions that can be developed into conditioned reflexes through concentration and persistent practise, and that can assist, therefore, in changing physical and mental states, in influencing self-esteem, and in controlling behaviour.

Intervention in the activity of organs is therefore possible, although it is a more difficult and complex process than the regulation of voluntary movements, especially since, unlike the former, the function of body organs is not trained in daily life. It seems both possible and reasonable to make conscious use of autosuggestion to the end of improving performance. But the process must be brought about in a sensible manner and with due regard for the relevant physiological and psychological laws.

The development of conditioned reflexes makes it possible to induce the blood to flow faster, the heart to beat slower, or the muscles to relax more quickly. Athletes can consciously learn to control their autonomic bodily functions through the use of PRTs. Just as Pavlov's dogs could be trained to salivate through conditioned response, so the ability of athletes to control their autonomic functions can be consciously learned. The thought, linguisitic, and imagination processes in the higher centres of the nervous system create links between autonomic and motor centres through conditioned reflexes; and these consciously influence both autonomic and motor functions.

The psycho-regulatory effect lies in a change in stimulation in the cells of the nervous system. The influence on the periphery is ensured by an increase in tonus in the parasympathetic system, which also leads to an acceleration in the recovery processes in the tissues. The tissues are then able to absorb and process a greater quantity of oxygen from the blood. Although blood circulation is slowed, the quantity of blood in the periphery is greater. The more complete utilization of oxygen by the tissues restores the energy potential of the working muscles more quickly, and the tissues are once again able to function more effectively. The nervous and muscle tissue, as well as the entire organism, recovers as a unified functional system.

An Overview of Psycho-Regulatory Techniques Used in Team Sports

An exhaustive classification of the PRTs used in sports will not be possible here. Instead, we will provide a general overview of the available procedures.

The PRTs may be classified into the following three areas, according to their physiological effects:

1. Psychological influencing of emotional and automatic processes by controlling the athlete's activity states—the most common techniques include:
  • autogenic training in sports;
  • psychotonic training;
  • concentration/relaxation training;
  • autogenic training using music.
2. Influencing of behaviours through contents of central information storage areas—the most commonly used techniques include:
  • ideomotor training;
  • mental training;
  • observational training;
  • stereotyped intention building (active therapy);
  • desensitization.
3. Limited procedure for physiological and psychological influencing (chiefly foreign suggestion), including:
  • relaxation procedures using biofeedback equipment;
  • application of music.

These procedures, which are given a closer examination in the next section, are presented in Diagram 12. Most of the procedures (with the exception of biofeedback and application of music) are based on autosuggestion. The advantage of this approach lies in the fact that once athletes have learned the techniques, they can use them actively and independently when needed. In

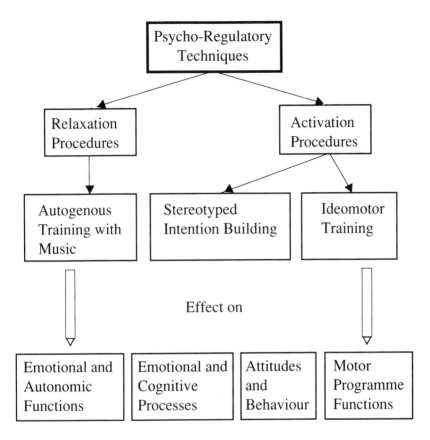

Diagram 12   Psycho-regulatory techniques used in team sports.

numerous cases the use of medication (e.g., sleeping pills) can be avoided, and a solid basis created for the rational use of psychoprophylaxy or psychotherapy.

2. Psycho-Regulatory Relaxation Techniques

Relaxation procedures allow players to relax between individual training units or competitive tasks, as well as to eliminate excessive competitive excitement or insomnia.

Some important prerequisites for successful application of these techniques are the following:

1. Athletes must participate in the program actively and voluntarily from the beginning. In the absense of a positive attitude toward the PRT, it will be difficult for the athlete to apply the technique successfully.

2. The PRT should be applied over a long period of time in training, especially in those stages where training is the most intensive. It is important that PRT be effective and that it be perceived as such by the athlete.

3. It is recommended that PRTs not be used until the procedure has been mastered. Again, the importance of maintaining a positive attitude in the athlete cannot be overestimated, and a necessary condition of maintaining a positive attitude is that the PRT not be applied carelessly or in a haphazard manner.

The psycho-regulatory techniques are useful only in interaction with other recovery methods, such as compensation training, proper diet, physiotherapy, massage, and making sports a part of one's life.

Autogenic Training with Application of Music

Autogenic training (AT) affects organic functions, which are controlled by the autonomic nervous system. By imagining relaxation intensively, the athlete can be put into a state of actual relaxation. If this imagination process is repeated frequently and systematically, the excited autonomic nervous centres of the brain are brought increasingly under conscious control. The relaxed state is brought about voluntarily.

The procedure can be learned by anyone, as long as the following conditions are observed:

- the athlete, as well as coaches, sports physicians, club officials, etc., must have   .
- positive attitude toward the procedure;
- the AT must be totally integrated into the training structure;
- the AT must be taught with careful attention to methodology and correct procedures; and
- favourable conditions must be maintained during the acquisiton process.

AT works through the repetition of simple sentences called formulae. The content of these sentences is imagined in concrete form, thereby creating a state of relaxation in the body.

The five basic formulae are

1. I am totally calm, totally relaxed.
2. Both of my arms are very heavy.
3. Both of my legs are very heavy.
4. Both of my arms are very warm.
5. Both of my legs are very warm.

Formulae or statements for other sports may differ according to the muscle groups used and as the particular characteristics of the athletes.

Acquisition of AT can take varying amounts of time. Typically the initial signs of relaxation are a feeling of heaviness and a prickling sensation in the fingers and muscle ends. If an athlete tries to master this technique too quickly, there is a serious risk that instead of relaxation inner tension will result.

Psycho-regulatory relaxation training (PRRT) using music is based on the same principle as the AT procedure. Before practising the formulae, relaxing music is played for appoximately three to four minutes (this is considered as external suggestion). Music harmonizes and makes athletes more receptive to verbal suggestion.

The prime purpose of this procedure is to promote rapid psycho-physical recovery following highly strenuous training and to compensate for overexertion.

The athlete assumes a relaxed position and concentrate on the music. Concentration alternates between the music and his or her physical self. After the music is played, the formulae for the AT (autosuggestive part) are introduced to the athlete. Of course, not every piece of music is suitable for this purpose. Very calm melodies in concerto form are preferred. In addition, they must be appropriate to the athlete's age and sex. This procedure is also used in groups and lasts approximately six to seven minutes.

The PRRT procedure is very useful in training. In many cases, athletes will already feel soothed and relaxed by the music, with conditioned reflexes already triggered. The following observations were obtained from the PRT procedure:

- Increased training intensity makes effective organization of psycho-physical recovery necessary in order for athletes to perform subsequent training units in a relaxed manner.
- The rapid succession of competitions in team sports also makes recovery necessary, especially when there is training between competitions.
- The PRRT procedure is good preparation for further psycho-regulatory

procedures, such as stereotyped intention building, ideomotor training, and others.

This relaxation program can successfully be used during half-time breaks. An example is provided below.

Application of Music during Half-Time Breaks in Soccer

After psycho-regulatory relaxation training with music has been introduced to a soccer team and implemented as a regular follow-up to intensive training, the question arises as to how this procedure can be effectively implemented during half-time as well. We discovered that there is in fact very little information in sports literature on the problems of half-time organization in soccer.

By observing the organization of various half-time breaks and by questioning coaches and athletes, we arrived at a rough structure for half-time breaks (see Diagram 13). This structure varies according to situations, such as distance from the playing field to the dressing rooms, and according to psychological factors, such as game score, spatial conditions, athletes' personalities, and coaches' characteristics.

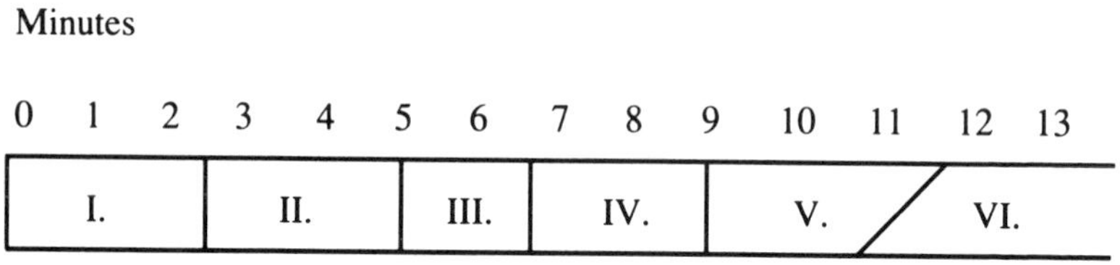

Minutes

Stages:

I. Leaving the playing field.
II. Freshening up, treatment.
III. Relaxation, music.
IV. Coaches' instructions to team.
V. Coaches' instructions to individual players.
VI. Warming up, entering the playing field.

Diagram 13   The structure of the time breaks in soccer.

The goal is to use half-time breaks in such a way that players are optimally prepared and motivated for the second half, that they do not repeat mistakes, and that they begin the second half of play in a high state of readiness.

Stage 1   Leaving the playing field.

At the beginning of the half-time break, players should proceed without delay to the dressing rooms. Along the way, players should take the opportunity to lower stimulation levels in their muscular systems by loosening up and/or doing aerobic exercises.

Stage 2   Freshening up, treatment.

Players freshen up, have a drink (tea, glucose, vitamins), change clothes, and receive treatment if necessary. After or during this time, each player assumes his or her position in the dressing room.

Stage 3   Relaxation, application of music.

This stage is particulary important from a psychological point of view. In order for the athletes to be able to take in the coach's instructions, they need an intensive relaxation stage. This can be supported by the coach's instructions to relax and breathe deeply.

Very good results also have been obtained with application of music during this stage. Relaxation music with a harmonious emotional effect is played for one and a half minutes. As players are able to master relaxation training, they will experience a subjectively beneficial state of relaxation. In addition, music acts as a diversion that allows players to collect and calm themselves. It becomes a true break.

Stage 4   Coach's instructions to the team.

Up to this point, the coach has an opportunity to reflect on what he/she should say during the half-time break. This time may be used to discuss points requiring special emphasis with colleagues or officials. The coach should, however, speak with the team alone, since it is his/her responsibility and it is this individual that has the confidence of the players.

The following psychological points must be observed:

• Do not give more than three pieces of information. It is unlikely that any more information will be assimilated. Make sure the information is relevant, precise, and unambiguous.

• Always begin with the positive. Praise always has a more stimulating and positive effect on performance than criticism. A mere recitation of the team's faults will be of little benefit. Say how it can be done better, drawing attention to the game flow and strategy of the opponent.

- Be brief and to the point. Those who do not understand what the coach has said will be unable to act on his advice.
- Be fair and do not offend anyone. Unfair comments, even if they are unintended, are divisive and tend to deplete collective spirit and competitive strength. Players' opinions are important, certainly. Let them have their say. But remember that you have seen the action from the outside, and that only you are in a position to give an informed and dispassionate assessment of the game.
- Summarize the important points. Emphasis improves retention. Again, draw attention to the strengths of the team.

Stage 5   Individual instructions.

Instructions which are meant for an individual player should not be given in front of the entire team. Telling everyone what concerns only one player serves merely to distract the team as a whole and to increase the likelihood that the other players will forget the information that is relevant to them. The fifth stage, in which players are preparing for the second half of the game, is the time to give special instructions to individual players. Coaching colleagues and officials may also be summoned to speak to individual players at this time. As before, give only the essential information; and when criticism must be given, always say immediately afterwards how it can be done better.

Stage 6   Warming up, entering the playing field.

On the way back to the playing field, each player should take the opportunity to warm up (calisthenics, flexibility, etc.) in order to be in peak performance state by the time play resumes.

Psycho-regulatory procedures may be used during the half-time break. However, these are only effective when used in conjunction with other measures; under no circumstances should they be used on their own.

3. Psycho-Regulatory Activation Techniques

Stereotyped Intention Building as Psychological Preparation for Competition

Where the application of relaxation procedures has the immediate desired effect and the athletes find themselves in a relaxed (drowsy) state, the physical exercises which immediately follow may be rendered less effective. It is therefore recommended that the procedures not be used before practice or competition. In order to reduce this disadvantage, various investigations were made to discover activation formulae for motivating athletes to reach optimal levels of readiness. Whereas relaxation procedures are directed more toward autonomic and emotional processes, activation motivation procedures are directed toward the cognitive processes, motor performance, attitudes, and behaviour.

Stereotyped intention building (SIB), which Frester (1) describes as being active therapy, promotes an optimistic competition-geared attitude in cases of self-doubt with opponents, referees, and one's own performance ability. Performance behaviour is motivated by requiring players to rapidly adapt to external conditions in competition, to mobilize all psychological and physical energies in the appropriate area, and to overcome initial difficulties more rapidly.

First, the reasons for incorrect attitudes and behaviour must be explained. Then, to enable athletes to identify with the goals that have been set, the main points in the task of intention building can be determined.

The principles behind the SIB sequence generally include the following steps:

Step 1   relaxation (AT): transition formula (depending on the sport and the objectives);

Step 2   psycho-physical activation (actual SI); and

Step 3   practical execution of exercise.

The formulae in step 2 must be determined individually and according to the sport in question. A few examples of such formulae are:
   – I am confident and self assured.
   – I am completely aware of my performance strength.
   – I am looking forward to the competition.
   Step 2 is followed by flexibility work.

Stereotyped intention building in team sports begins when there are no other tasks to be completed before the upcoming competition. In general, the process begins seven days before the game. Once or twice a day, in conjunction with relaxation training, the procedure directs athletes' concentration toward the main aspects of the game, and important instructions are given in the form of formulae that reinforce the coach's ideas and direct the players's attention to the specific requirements of the game.

Players are readily able to imagine these formulae in the form of concrete situations, and as a result of mentally occupying themselves with their tasks, are better able to concentrate directly and pedagogically on the game.

It is understandably difficult to prove the effects of the SIB procedure, as it is only one method among several and is not a deciding factor. It is generally believed, however, that this procedure psychologically prepares players for competition.

Ideomotor Training for Perfecting and Stabilizing Technique and Tactics

(1) In ideomotor training (IT), thought and imagination processes regarding movement in sports are stressed. The IT procedure speeds up the acquisition of new skills, the ability to retrain, and the stabilization of selected skills; (2) promotes retention of training during the active relaxation process or while players are not practising due to injury or sickness; (3) reduces fear and inhibitions in executing certain motor skills; and (4) concentrates the athletes' mood exclusively on the movement sequence of the game.

The IT procedure affects each player differently. For this reason, their athletic experiences, abstraction abilities, responsibilities, emotional states, and attitudes should be considered. The coach and athlete will determine the content and sequence of the IT procedure, and establish the formulae together. Important details will be stressed in order to increase the athlete's information retention. These formulae should be expressed in terms readily comprehensible to the athlete.

The IT procedure is particularly effective when the internal actualization of a movement image is followed by the actual external execution of the movement. The following practice plan has been proved successful:

a. initial relaxation phase - internal actualization;
b. ideomotor training phase - internal actualization;
c. movement execution phase - external relaxation.

Athletes should learn these basically simple, completely innocuous methods (like all PRTs) in order to combat high levels of physical and psychological stress. Of course, these methods will not compensate for shortcomings in training. They must be an integral part of training, like the other PRTs.

The potential of PRT programmes to improve performance has not yet been realized. Intensive work is being done all over the world to combine and to perfect the various procedures. The application of psycho-regulatory activation

Talent is the principle criterion on the basis of which children are selected from the population as a whole for specialized training. Talent criteria are based on the structure and specific demands and characteristics of the respective sport and on the child's age, psychological profile, and motor development.

procedures, for example, is now being tested for correct tactical behaviour.

An example of the psychological technique in standard situations in soccer is presented below.

The main challenge to the use of the IT procedure in soccer is that, practically speaking, no situation has exactly the same motor execution. The influence of opponents, teammates, tactical solutions, and ball movements create new and unpredictable variations, making it considerably more difficult to imagine motor sequences. There are, however, certain situations in soccer which are relatively stable, such as penalty kicks, corner kicks, free kicks, etc.

The IT programme was tested on one soccer team using the free kick variation. Although this work is still unfinished and a number of important questions remain unanswered, the method and procedure are illustrated here to call attention to the potential applications.

The following steps have been suggested:

Step 1 Exploration and elaboration of the free kick variation.
The coach determined three variations with three players for the free kick situation, left or right, in the penalty area (20 m).

Step 2 Verbalization of the motor sequence.
The actions for each player (A, B, C) were then presented verbally and graphically.

Step 3 Explanation of the variations.
Variations were explained to the players during during practice.

Step 4 Practical execution of movements.
Players practised the variations until they had mastered the motor sequence completely.

Step 5 Analysis of motor sequence.
The strengths and weaknesses of execution were assessed by questioning each player of his performance and by observation of performance characteristics.

Step 6 Development of IT formulae.
The main strengths and weaknesses were determined and verbalized in formulae in consultation with each individual player.

Step 7 Application of IT programme.
Players now train individually using their IT programme (internal actualization). Before executing each movement, they first concentrate with the aid of their programmes.

Step 8 Revision.
By continually monitoring players (by use of video equipment) the IT procedure can be continually revised.

One training variation utilized on the team is demonstrated in Diagram 14. This method proved to be effective in practice. All of the free kicks played according to this variation in the last game were successful, although the shots on goal were not always successful in every case. Technique, tactics, fitness, and especially training, which are inextricably linked with the IT procedure, all influence athletic performance.

The IT procedure leads to a better mental image of standard situations and

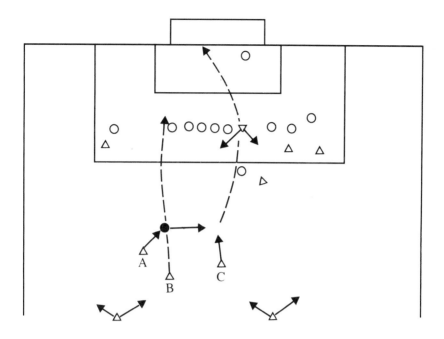

Player A

1. I am standing near the ball.
2. After B has started, I will play diagonally to C.

Player B

1. I place the ball on the free kick point.
2. I take a run up.
3. I run powerfully over the ball and move in.

Player C

1. I take a quick but powerful run-up.
2. I give the ball a powerful kick past the wall and into the left corner.

Diagram 14   Ideomotor training of a free kick variation.

a more conscious and deliberate approach to execution. Where video equipment is available to monitor the IT procedure, the effectiveness of the method can be very accurately guaged and precise modifications to individual programs made accordingly.

4. Evaluation of the Effectiveness of Psycho-Regulatory Techniques

Psycho-regulatory training cannot be learned in a day or be measured with a yardstick. The PRTs help athletes gradually achieve new psycho-emotional levels; and when PRTs are made a regular part of training, they appear quite natural. Nevertheless, many attempts have been made to measure the effect of PRTs from physiological, psychological as well as performance viewpoints.

The physiological methods require the use of equipment, and for this reason, cannot be used everywhere. The principle methods are:

1. measuring skin temperature;
2. measuring heart rate (also ECG);
3. measuring skin resistance;
4. electromyography;
5. electroencephalography.

Psychological methods include:

1. written assessment using structured questionnaires of effects experienced by athletes during the learning process and after practice;
2. oral questions;
3. observations.

The performance criteria requires comparisons of performance results obtained before and after the use of PRTs using statistical analysis, such as t-tests or subjective evaluation. It is also possible to study the changes in performance of a control group (no use of PRTs) in comparison to an experimental group of players (application of PRTs). In order to obtain adequate information about the effects of the PRTs, procedures for evaluation of the effects must be as thorough and precise as possible. This ensures that a wide range of the procedural effectiveness is noted and recorded and that all the different reactions of individual athletes are taken into consideration.

CHAPTER 11

Talent Identification in Team Sports

1. Introduction

Work in the field of talent identification among East German sports psychologists is broadly conceived within the context of what is called the "socialist personality." The socialist personality may be defined, very roughly, as that personality type which conforms to the needs, goals, and expectations of the socialist state. Such a personality would, in theory at least, place a high value on the "collective," on the importance of teamwork, and on the value of sports as a social institution. The socialist personality profile, in turn, is formed on the basis of what is called the "typical personality." The typical personality is the material out of which, as it were, the socialist personality is formed. It contains—only in the abstract, of course—all the features which are deemed objective constituents of personality: perseverance, toughness, timidity, self-reliance, moderation, and so on. In developing the socialist personality, then, one attempts to incorporate and, indeed, to develop to the fullest extent, those personality characteristics that are thought intrinsically desirable to the society. Given the very strict division of labour under socialism, talent identification becomes the conscious and deliberate promotion of those whose personality profiles are best suited to contributing to socialism in a particular way. None other than Lenin himself has said that the purpose of talent identification is "to lead the majority of working people to an actual field of activity where they can distinguish themselves, where their abilities can unfold; to reveal those talents which the people bring forth like an inexhaustible source (6:402)."

Talent identification is, for these reasons, characterized by East German sports psychologists as a uniquely humanistic pursuit; that is to say, it is characterized as an activity that has as its central goal the perfection of the human personality. In socialist terms, it aims to optimize the relationship between the social and the individual, and it seeks to furnish every individual with a sense of self worth, based on their abilities and skills.

The extension of this general conception of talent identification to sports is not difficult to see. Where, in respect to those abilities requisite to a particular sport, an individual shows great promise, every opportunity must be given to afford them free expression for the good of the state. Talent identification in sports is merely a means of expediting this process, of making possible the fullest expression of an individual's talent in respect to a particular sport. Three points are particularly emphasized:

1. When talent in sports is successfully developed in international levels, the societal and political function of sports becomes very important.
2. Personal needs and interests are met as the successful athlete realizes his or her personality potential.
3. A reliable prediction of aptitude or talent in a certain sports allows correct individual decisions and minimizes setbacks in individual development.

It may be concluded that aptitude diagnosis makes it possible to carry out a long term organization of individual education and training for athletic development.

Talent identification is defined as the evaluation of an individual's performance prerequisites and performance expectations, both of which are important for successfully meeting present and future athletic demands.

There is an interaction between performance prerequisites and demand. The markedness levels of the complex individual performance prerequisites govern aptitude as well as demands. Accordingly, aptitude diagnosis is both a selection process and a training principle. Aptitude diagnosis assessments are a prognostic assessment, as they make it possible to predict probable future performance ability.

2. Athletic Components of Talent/Identification in Team Sports

In sports, talent identification is carried out by means of a system that consists of scouting, testing, and identifying of talented children. Talent is the principle criterion on the basis of which children are selected from the population as a whole for specialized training. Talent criteria are based on the structure and specific demands and characteristics of the respective sport and on the child's age, psychological profile, and motor development.

Even in the case of individual sports, where performance structure and corresponding aptitude criteria are less complex than in team sports, the number of relevant criteria are nonetheless adequate to make a reliable identification of talent. Fitness and anthropometric criteria are deemed to be the most important factors in these instances; they, in themselves, are thought to be quite sufficient to maintain the integrity of the talent identification process.

Psychological and technical criteria, however, are more complex than fitness and anthropometric criteria. Accordingly, in those sports whose performance is determined largely by psychological and technical criteria, aptitude diagnosis is complex and interdisciplinary.

In team sports, which are highly complex, this demand must be stressed even more. Here, talent identification involves three factors: (1) determination of complex game performance through observation; (2) individual performance parameters; and (3) health and scholastic achievement.

The decisive factor in determining the level to which a talent is developed, however, is still the information gained in competition, youth"spartakiads", and championships. Even here, talent identification remains a highly subjective procedure and requires considerable experience and knowledge on the part of coaches, trainers, teachers, and so on. The results obtained from observations must be supported by an assessment of individual performance parameters. We know that fitness and technical parameters are determined by assessment tests; but tactical parameters are not susceptible in the same way to precise examination. There are no measurable parameters which would enable us to judge these specific components of athletic performance.

We know that a decisive criterion for determining talent in team sports is playing ability. This complex performance component plays a decisive role both in training and competition. But, although playing ability is the predominant criterion for assessing talent in team sports, this component, as well as condition and constitution, has a significance which changes relative to the team sport in question (e.g., soccer, volleyball, basketball, etc.).

Our next analysis attempts to specify the role of talent identification in team sports, taking into consideration the significance of playing ability. We shall take particular note of the ways in which the measurability of components of playing ability can be improved.

3. The Concept of Playing Ability in Team Sports

In order to elaborate on procedures for assessing playing ability, a uniform working definition of the concept is required. For this purpose an analysis of the performance structure of team sports is necessary. Technique and tactics are crucial components of the performance structure, a structure which includes both psychological (sensory, intellectual, and psycho-motor) and physical (motor and fitness) performance factors. Specific psychological, fitness, and motor factors are all evident in the definition of playing ability according to current views. We therfore find that such concepts as game ability, game intelligence, game effectiveness, and playing ability, as well as concrete definitions for the concept of playing ability are used synomously. Thiess (12) considers playing ability to be an expression of anticipation ability; whereas Mahlo (8) views it as a complex of individual skills and the ability to effectively utilize these skills.

On the basis of the above discussion, and taking into consideration the factors in game activity which determine performance, we propose the following definition of playing ability: it is a complex ability which tactically combines a multitude of psychological and physical abilities, as well as a host of technical skills, with complex game manoeuvres in such a way that the required task is solved in the most effective way (12:203).

Playing ability is the prerequisite for game performance. Diagram 15 shows the position of playing ability in its essential relation to other performance prerequisites. It is influenced by specific psychological and physical performance prerequisites. Among the psychological performance prerequisities, the intellectual factor affects tactical behaviour directly; whereas the sensory and psycho-motor abilities (which are not clearly psychologically governed) influence tactics through physical and fitness performance. As well as having a moderating function, character and will power traits have an important role in the development of performance prerequisites. Tactics are the integral link and are expressed in playing ability which, in turn, is the prerequisite for game performance. Game performance, when evaluated in terms of game effectiveness, does not allow for any reliable predictions about the levels of playing ability.

Goals and Tasks of Specialized Disciplines in Determining Playing Ability

The concrete goal of aptitude testing in sports is to examine and to determine the interaction between individual psychological and physical performance prerequisites, on the one hand, and the specific demands made during the execution of a game play, on the other. Two specialized disciplines, sports methodology and sports psychology, are particularly useful in this endeavour. The two discipline, although related, are not identical. The tasks of sports methodology lie primarily in the phenomenal level, since game actions are the evident result

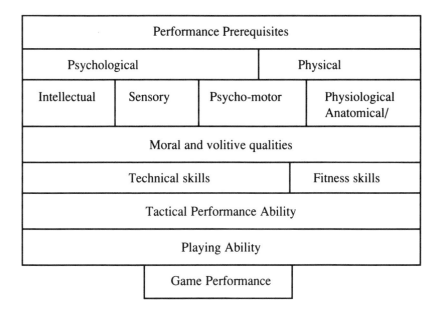

Diagram 15   Playing ability and its relationship with performance prerequisites and game performance.

of the interaction between performance prerequisities and demands. Accordingly, the tasks of sports methodology are found chiefly in the following two areas:

1. The first task consists of recording those game actions which determine playing ability and of determining the valency of game actions for playing ability.
2. The second task consists of devising and implementing procedures for the individual diagnosis of game manoeuvre execution ability, and from this, of game ability overall.

The tasks of sports psychology, on the other hand, help determine psychological traits which are quite likely responsible for an athlete's playing ability. Investigations are being carried out to determine which psychological performance prerequisites are necessary for the execution of game manoeuvres. It is strongly believed that psychological performance prerequisites are indispensible for the execution of game manoeuvres. They are primarily of a casual nature and cannot be analysed directly, but only on the basis of a measurement of behaviour.

4. Talent Identification Methodology in Team Sports

Methodological aspects which are fundamental to talent identification and which apply subsequently to methodological work in team sports are:

• Aptitude diagnosis in personality testing: In both middle class aptitude diagnosis and in industrial psychology, the trend is to reduce aptitude diagnosis to "pure" performance diagnosis. Here, the individual is seen exclusively as a producer of actions. This dualism of performance and personality traits is not consistent with the Marxist concept of unity of the personality (5).

• Aptitude diagnosis is developmental or process diagnosis. The personality is viewed as dynamic, not static; i.e., it is constantly subject to processes of development. Aptitude diagnosis must be considered in the developmental aspect of personality traits. It must be carried out during the correct stage of development, in order to avoid misleading conclusions about development which is either particularly effective or very unsatisfactory in nature. As is well known, there are the so-called "favourable development stages" during the course of motor development. This fact must be recognized when interpreting the research results.

• Talent identification and training form a single unit. The task of aptitude diagnosis is to diagnose personality traits which develop during the training process. A knowledge of the individual markedness levels of these traits is necessary for the optimal structuring of individual training and education. It is imperative, therefore, to include aptitude testing in the training process.

The Marxist image of humans, which is neither static nor fatalistic, forms the basis of the methodological approach referred to above. The product of this fundamental concept, i.e., the diagnostic determination of the development process, is also important. A diagnosis of this type must, in principle, be carried out from two different perspectives. On the one hand, one must record the individual development process quantitatively over specific periods of time. On the other hand, one must examine the nature of the individual development process qualitatively over specific intervals of time. With regard to the quantitative aspects, the principle aim is to study differences between the variations of the pre- and post-test results. The researcher must also recognize, however, that factors unrelated to the experiment may have an effect on performance growth between the two testings. Usually, these factors are difficult to control.

Individual Methodological Steps

A. The Analysis of Demand and Behaviour

The first methodological step is to thoroughly analyse the motor actions/ behaviour that constitute a player's ability (3). This is the particular domain of sports methodology. To analyse these actions, film and video recordings are used, as well as consultation with experts.

Motor analyses form the basis of an analysis of the demands found in the psychological and physical sphere. Psychology and medicine must therefore deduce the performance prerequisites which are necessary for motor execution (see example in Diagram 16).

The well-known personality and behavioural models (5) designed to measure fundamental characteristics for playing ability are taken from psychology. The classification of actions and behaviour and their characteristics is made with the aid of expert opinions and observations. This results in the development of a psychological demand profile (psychogramme), which contains the identified psychological performance prerequisites relevant to playing ability and their valencies.

Many problems arise in the elaboration of the analysis of demands. The demand problem is very complex. Not only is the number of demand characteristics large, but the relationships between them, numerous and complex. This means that the chances of compensating for specific poorly developed characteristics with better developed ones are relatively good. However, it is rarely possible to compensate for characteristics with a high valency in the demand profile. This must be considered in the evaluation of individual playing ability, as well as in the talent identification process.

B. Construction and Validation of Aptitude Tests

The identified motor actions, patterns, and manoeuvres, and the determined demands of individual team sports, form the basis for construction of aptitude tests. The main emphasis is then placed on the structure and validation of tests in sports methodology.

The following aptitude tests for sports methodology have been developed and

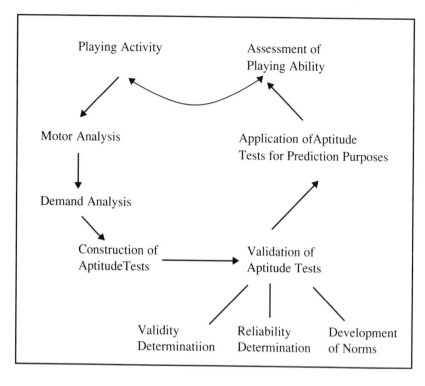

Diagram 16   Methodical steps in talent identification work based on playing ability.

validated:

Film Procedure This procedure consists of showing a film containing approximately 20 game situations which are interrupted in pre-determined section so that the test subject may find the best solution. This test primarily records the player's ability to solve given game situations in a creative manner.

Slide Procedure In this procedure, basic game combinations with possible individual and collective solutions are shown in an abstract and vivid manner in the form of colour slides. Each situation is accompanied by four to five possible solutions, one of which is the best. This procedure makes it possible to determine the player's abstraction ability when solving given situations.

Questionnaires Questionnaires are designed to determine tactical knowledge of players. They are age-specific, based on the demands of play, and ask questions on the knowledge of rules, as well as on the individual and collective tactical principles behind attacking and defensive plays.

The following tests are used in sports psychology:

Peglau's (1) Multi-Variable Perception Test (MPT) This test examines the accuracy and speed of visual perception. Specific signals which must be recognized quickly and accurately are given at high speeds to the players.

Konzak's Distributive and Focused Attention Test This test was developed to differentiate athletes according to their ability to distribute or focus attention. It also measures the athlete's ability to switch attention rapidly from one object to another. This test includes performance demands that make possible a comparison between measurable single task and multiple task performances. Simple mental tasks, such as calculation and simple reaction performance to simple and complex stimuli, are used. (The test was described in detail in Chapter 3.)

Intellectual Ability Test The test is designed to determine intellectual abilities in athletes. It is based on similar tests developed earlier by Horn (4) and Raven (11).

Will-Power Test This test was designed to measure the athlete's will-power qualities. It is based on the Pauli test (9).

5. Practical Implications of Talent Recognition and Selection

The central thesis, that the process talent recognition is one which is susceptible of scientific precision, can be proven only in practice. But the practical test must be informed by theoretical considerations at every stage. This ensures that the unity between talent identification and training methodology remains intact. Bearing in mind that junior training is always talent recognition training, the content of what is taught must be made more precise. In this way, it becomes possible to judge the talent of young players during the course of aptitude and selection processes. Last, and most important, the presence or absence of talent should be judged in the transition to regular training. In order to achieve this objective, all of the procedures presented above are combined into a test battery. In addition to this test battery, other testing methods for evaluation of fitness and

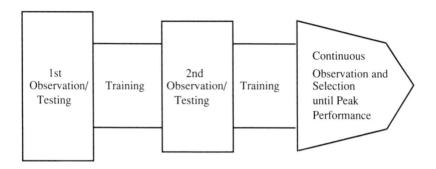

Diagram 17   Longitudinal process of aptitude testing from the start of one's sports training career to reaching peak performance.

technical skills will remain components of the talent examination.

The assessment of an individual's general aptitude for a particular team sports activity begins at the moment the first step toward selection is made. For this, standard procedures are used; a player's playing ability is determined first by reference to game reports. A closer examination is then made in the specific selection process. The reports obtained from game observations are then compared to test results. In training, further tests are carried out at regular intervals by the respective sport governing bodies and clubs. These tests of playing ability are sport and age specific. Judgements are then made about performance levels and the development potential of talented players. This does not mean, however, that playing ability is no longer the subject of investigation; it remains a fundamental criterion of selection at higher levels of performance. The methods of talent identification here proposed open up new possibilities for the further improvement of performance diagnosis. Diagram 17 schematically illustrates the longitudinal process of testing and selection of athletes for high level performance.

CHAPTER 12

Educational Methodology in Team Sports in the German Democratic Republic

1. Educational Methods

Although a number of scientific papers have been published on education methodology, there is still no unified classification of methods for the education of athletes. One reason for this may be in the various fundamental bases for classification. Ogordonikov (8) appears to have arrived at a suitable subdivision. His procedure corresponds to the usual classification found in specialized Soviet literature, which distinguishes between persuasion on the one hand, and methods for organizing and conducting the daily activities and behaviour of the upcoming generation on the other. The fundamental theory of this classification is represented by two closely related major trends in education. Makarenko (7) characterizes the first one as the trend from "awareness to behaviour," and the second, as the trend from "behaviour to awareness." The decisive factors in the development of awareness and behaviour are instruction, experience, persuasion, and habitation.

Instruction leads to the acquisition of an educationally relevant cultural heritage. In order for education to be effective, the knowledge which is acquired must be complemented and supported by an individual's own experiences. For this purpose, experiences must be organized into a framework of activity. The personality is thus developed through what is portrayed as a "dialectical unity" between instruction and experience.

Persuasion and habituation are closely related to instruction and the organization of experience. Players become accustomed to correct behaviour through instruction and the establishment of norms and demands. Socially acceptable behaviour must be internalized. Players' personality is shaped and organized by practising standard behaviour.

Methods of persuasion include educational methods which impart an educationally relevant cultural heritage. Their effectiveness depends on the degree of correspondence between acquired knowledge and personal experience. Those educational methods which lead to correct behaviour through practice and the establishment of norms are a part of the system of methods and habituation. Methods of persuasion direct awareness to behaviour; methods of habituation transform behaviour into awareness.

Since the goal of education is the unity between awareness and behaviour, both the methods of persuasion and of habituation are important. Neglecting either aspect will inhibit personality development.

Knowledge acquired empirically forms the basis for the development of convictions. There are a number of different ways to teach an educationally relevant cultural heritage.

In team sports, knowledge in the DDR is acquired primarily within the framework of Free German Youth Organization meetings as well as theory classes. During instruction, all statements must be proven. This is done mainly using concrete, easy-to-remember examples from practice. Burdzisch (1) suggested the following methodological principles for teaching and learning:

1. presentation and assimilation of the scientific statements;
2. proof of all statements;
3. evaluation of the statements by the athletes; and
4. assessments of athletes' actions and behaviour (how these can be related to the statements).

These individual methodological steps are complemented and supported by the athletes' personal experiences. In many situations, however, experiences can also have an inhibitory, negative influence, as is the case when negative experiences are compounded with shaky knowledge. On the other hand, positive experiences often compensate for a lack of knowledge and can lead to the formation of strong valuable convictions.

In order for specific sport knowledge to become highly effective, educational methodology, such as pedagogical discussions and educational instructions, are necessary. These methods, which are used in all areas of life, shape the consciousness and morals of athletes and are a part of the system of methods that are designed to build convictions. Discussions and educational instructions help to expose and resolve the discrepancies that may arise in an athlete's required and actual behaviour, in his or her knowledge, and in his or her actions.

Private discussions with the coach or small group discussions are used to determine the causes of behavioural problems in general and to change them. Educational instruction, in contrast to discussion, is based more on actions and behaviour which adhere to the norm. Discussions primarily lead to greater team effectiveness. They are an important method of forming convictions and attitudes when specific pedagogical and, in this context, collective prerequisites are present.

The methods of habituation, whose main emphasis is obedience to given norms and rules, require coaches to use such methodological forms as direct and indirect behaviour practice and the distribution of short and long term tasks.

When following and implementing standard educational methodology, educators must consider specific complex principles such as demands and evaluation, praise and criticism, etc.

Demands have a decisive effect on the education of athletes. They lead to considerable conflicts in personality development. At first, the pedagogical demands which are aimed at objectively important goals lead to the creation of an external conflict between required actions and behaviour and the actual action and behavioural levels of the athlete. When an athlete accepts demands, an inner conflict results which triggers actions and behaviour in accordance with the demands and which aids in the development of his or her personality.

These inner conflicts are the actual driving forces behind development. They can transform various social influences into specific positive changes in personality.

The formation and dissolution of conflicts which result from making and fulfilling demands become the central factor in a socialistic upbringing. It has already been stressed that an inner conflict will not appear until the demand has been accepted by the individual. Before athlete accepts the demand, he or she must verify what is required, whether it can be achieved, and whether it is beneficial or useful.

To influence the acceptance of demands positively, coaches must consider the following:

• Demands which have already been completely justified within the framework of education and training, and which have become norms for athletic activity, must be consistently implemented without discussion. Stolz (15) makes a distinction here between categorical demands, actions, and behaviour deemed worthwhile by society, and the strongest type of demand, which is often associated with punishment or the threat of punishment.

• Demands must be justified logically to the team or the individual, especially within the framework of conviction building activities. On the logic of demands, Makarenko concludes: "I fear being illogical. I devised the following personal basic principle for myself: I never made demands if I was not sure whether they were correct or not. I waited for an opportunity when it was obvious to myself and to anyone with common sense that I was right. Then I made dictatorial demands, right down to the last player and, since they proved to be good demands because of the evident truth, I appeared bolder. The children saw that I was right and followed my instructions quickly" (7:156). Makarenko's statement is valid for all areas of a socialist upbringing. Before athletes can accept a demand, they must know why the demand is being made. They must be shown that the demand is correct and useful.

• Demands must always be directed towards the highest performance levels of an athlete without becoming unreasonable. Demands which are excessive, in most cases, lead to resignation. However, if the demand is too easy, there is no conflict between what is required and what presently exists. Personality development is consequently not ensured and the athlete may become bored.

• Demands must be clear and unequivocal. They should be made objectively so that mutual respect is maintained between educators and students.

• Demands should be supported, if possible, by suitable levels of motivation. Athletes must repeatedly be made aware of their performance goals and the type of recognition they will receive if these goals are successfully met.

A decisive factor in the acceptance of demands is the nature of the relationship between the coach and athletes. This will be discussed in greater detail later.

In order for demands to be met, the scope and quality of the demand must be determined. Not only must assessments check performance and record errors, they must examine the causes of shortcomings and determine how to eliminate them. Coaches should assess the actions and behaviour recorded in test results and should evaluate the results from the point of view of societal demands. Coaches should be able to compare the actual and required action and behaviour by means of these assessments and thus to determine an athlete's development potential. Evaluations will have a greater educational value when (a) they are oriented towards class-structured education; (b) they are correct and the athletes recognize these evaluations as such; and (c) athletes are able to assess themselves objectively.

On the basis of these evaluations, coaches praise or criticize. Fair praise and criticism is very important. Excessive praise or unjust criticism will not be recognized by the team members, and the coach will lose his authority. We often observe that praise, with its highly stimulating effect on performance and behaviour, is dispensed too seldom; on the other hand, criticism is used too often and, instead of solving conflicts, causes new ones.

2. Responsibilities of Coaches in the Education of Athletes

The main responsibility for the implementation of an educational methodology on teams is the coach. The leadership role and the contact with the athletes makes him or her the most qualified person to exert an educational influence. When abilities and experience are used effectively, the coach's influence on the athletes' actions and behaviour can be considerable, and perhaps greater than the influence of any other educator in a parallel domain. A coach's success in education involves many factors. These include personal qualities as well as leadership skills. Coaches also need a comprehensive knowledge of educational processes, goals, methods, organizational principles; and need to know the personalities of his or her athletes, the characteristics of their inner states, and of the social demands and tasks that will be required of them. If coaches lack this knowledge, any goal-oriented, conscious educational influence they might have on their players is limited from the start. On the other hand, the knowledge which was described above is by itself no guarantee of success in education. For this purpose, a series of educational prerequisites is required. First of all, however, we will list a few characteristics required of coaches in the GDR (10).

1. Coaches must possess a clear fundamental political and ideological position, a political perspective, as it were, which permeates their entire thought and feeling processes. His/her actions and behaviour must totally reflect the interests of the working class and party, socialistic ideology and patriotism, and proletarian internationalism. Political and ideological knowledge is as essential for this position as comprehensive experience.

2. Coaches must be distinguished in pedagogical training. They must also express their convictions and demands. Those who want to inspire others must themselves be inspired; they must be able to get the attention of others and keep it. Thus Scurkova (13:918) writes of the moral "I" of the pedagogue: it "exists" for those whose education they are responsible, exclusively in their reactions, views, words, contact with others, manners, and behaviour. The moral "I" of the pedagogue must be emotional and enthusiastic; it must grip others, so they become "the same way." Feelings will have no effect unless they are expressed emotionally and enthusiastically.

3. Coaches must possess a comprehensive knowledge of their sport. A specialized knowledge of one's subject is of critical importance in making the right decisions during training. It determines how training is organized, how training apparata are used, and how competitive plans are established. This knowledge, however, is not enough in itself. A good general knowledge is also essential in training and competition.

4. Coaches' attitudes toward the education and training of athletes is fundamental to the example they will set for their players. Coaches require a great sense of responsibility and conscientiousness to encourage responsible and conscientious attitudes and behaviour from their players in competition.

5. Coaches must express strength of character and will in their manners and behaviour. Coaches who conduct the education and training processes in this way, whose behaviour in every situation is morally impeccable, develop in others by means of the example they set, the moral qualities and psychological traits that are most desirable for their sport.

6. A desire to complete a general education is also important for coaches. A high level of general education is necessary in all educators for the all-round development of the personalities entrusted to their care. A coach who concentrates solely on sports and ignores the other interests of his players will have a negative effect on performance. Only when coaches have acquired an adequate general education will they be in a position to influence and have a positive effect on the numerous interests of their players. Relationships between coach and athlete, which are very important for training and education, are frequently established on the basis of common interests.

Those qualities that go into making the personality profile of the coach well-rounded must be found in equal measure in the personality profile of the athletes under their care. Coaches set an example for their players and encourage them in their personality development. Coaches can have a negative influence on the team and can lose authority if their behaviour is not up to standard.

Needless to say, even a coach whose behaviour is exemplary will have great difficulty if he/she does not have a good relationship with the players. This relationship is largely determined by the pedagogical and methodological procedures at hand and by the coach's leadership style (6). Below, some of the more important principles of the coach-athlete relationship (12) are outlined.

First principle: be a partner and a friend.
This is the first and most important principle. It creates the basis for solid trust between athlete and coach. Being a partner and a friend means giving the athletes

---

Coaches can achieve and maintain a high performance through persistence and consistency and by following an established programme. The personality profiles and performance levels of athletes will develop and improve considerably if the coach sets a good example.

recognition, listening to their opinions, understanding their problems, including the athletes in the organization of education and training, and trusting them. By including the athletes as partners, they become able to identify with the tasks and objectives of competitive sports. They also feel more responsible for the process which they have helped shape and are unwavering in their opinions and value judgements of these processes.

Second principle: be honest.
This principle is closely related to the first. All decisions which affect the athlete, as well as performance and behavioural assessments, must be discussed openly. If an athlete learns of a coach's critical attitude toward him/her from others, the relationship of trust will be considerably weakened. A coach can only expect honesty and openness from the athletes if he is prepared to exhibit these same characteristics himself. Authority can be maintained and, indeed, increased.

Third principle: be persistent and consistent.
Continuously higher performance demands and objectives require coaches to be persistent and consistent. The fulfillment of tasks must never tolerate a lowering of expectations. Coaches can achieve and maintain a high performance through persistence and consistency and by following an established programme. The personality profiles and performance levels of athletes will develop and improve considerably if the coach sets a good example.

Fourth principle: have high demands.
The fast and sometimes astonishingly rapid performance development which has been present in most sports for several years means that continued success can be achieved only if even higher demands are made on the athletes. We may assume that there is a law-governed relationship between steadily increasing demands and performance growth. Coaches who make the highest demands possible of their athletes and carry them through within the framework of the pedagogical process, ensure the continued performance and personality growth of their athletes. The degree that the principles described here are closely intertwined is shown by, among other things, the fact that high demands can only be carried through effectively when there is a relationship of trust and friendship between coach and athlete. Coaches who present their demands in a determined and consistent manner, and who do not deviate from them when they are justified, even in the case of failure, will set a good example.

Over or undertaxing players, however, will diminish the authority of the coach, and athletes will lose faith in his/her expertise. For this reason, coaches must set demands very near the athletes' best performance level without surpassing it. This requires a great deal of experience, expert knowledge, and close collaboration with sports sciences.

Fifth principle: justify commands.
Good performance requires the creative and active participation of the athletes. Without such participation, long term goals could not be reached. A coach whose activity is based on authoritarianism and reglementation will drain the strength and inner resources of the athletes. Athletes must understand why certain demands and tasks are necessary. Justification should not be used, however, after demands have become norms. These norms should be carried out in a persistent manner with the appropriate measure of inflexibility.

Sixth principle: offer constructive criticism.
Constructive criticism is also of major significance in sports. Criticism should never serve as an end in itself; it must aim at appropriate changes in athletes' actions and behaviour. In order for criticism to be constructive, it must be fair, objective, convincing, and take into consideration the age and personality of the athlete. Coaches who are self-critical will be good examples to their teams. By example, they will encourage athletes to judge their own performance critically. Coaches who reject justified criticism will have difficulty instilling a true sense of constructive criticism and in maintaining a constructively critical atmosphere on the team.

Seventh principle: create feeling of success.
Feelings of success are triggered in athletes by praise and recognition; these feelings have a stimulating effect on their behaviour and actions. It is irrelevant if these feelings are made in the wake of tremendous athletic achievements, or if they are organized within the framework of the pedagogical process. Activity which has been praised will be repeated by the athlete and continued with even greater intensity. Athletes will look forward to further feeling of success, or praise.

The stimulating performance potential of praise and recognition from coach must be used in a conscious and purposeful manner. When utilized properly, athletes' actions and behaviour will be influenced in the desired manner. Praise and recognition from the coach, and the respect they convey, will have a positive effect on the trust between coach and athlete.

3. The Team's Education

The dynamics of the group is itself a decisive factor in the effectiveness of educational methodology. "The members of a group are joined by a common activity for the fulfillment of the same general objective and by the ensuing responsibility and friendly cooperation. The team performs a task best through the cooperation of each team member in fulfilling an activity appropriate to his/her ability. This system of roles contributes to education and self-discipline in the group, and therefore to personality development" (16:125).

Makarenko, the founder of collective education, portrays collectivity as the primary method of influencing individuals in education. Many examples occur in practice. Since the education of the personality requires a specific level of collective development, the development of the collectivity must be the first goal of any pedagogical work. The following section, using the example of attitude development, illustrates the significance of targeted influencing of the team and by the team.

Hiebsch and Vorwerg (4) provide us with the basic theoretical starting points for the group tasks and the position held by the group in the development of attitudes. Both scientists prove in their study on cooperative activity that attitudes constitute "a willingness to react with certain groups in concrete situations with a certain amount of inevitability and compulsoriness." It represents "above all, as a socio-psychological fact, a tendency of individuals to depend upon the norms of the group" (4). As is proven in educational practice, only those attitudes which correspond to the norms and beliefs of the group or collectivity will blossom.

Individuals who behave in a manner which deviates from the group norm or collective ideology will not be accepted by the group. The desire to conform with the norms and values of the group can be observed among athletes in all sports and disciplines. Since, however, competitive performance in team sports is "not only an individual result, but also the product of planned and effective teamwork during the course of competition by a group of athletes who continually come into contact with each other" (2:30), it can be concluded that the tendency towards conformity is more prominent in team sports than in individual sports. In team sports, individual players can jeopardize the group's objective with improper actions and behaviour, and render ineffective the actions of the others. In this respect, the demands and compulsion of team players to comply with the group norms are greater than in a group of athletes in individual sports (11). A well-developed team whose norms comply with social and pedagogical objectives has, for this reason, a host of educational advantages.

The attitude of the team, however, does not always correspond to the objective. The advantages of team sports over individual sports can also become disadvantages. For example, certain learning methods are rejected by sports teams because the group believes these forms of training are notimportant to performance development. Athletes who originally had a positive attitude toward these methods now quickly change their opinions to the opinions of the incorrect group ideology.

The building of positive attitudes through groups comes about primarily by means of socially acceptable demands which meet specific goals. These goals are conveyed to each individual member by the team. The establishment and dissolution of conflicts described earlier aids in personality deavelopment. The desire to conform ensures that the norms imposed by the group are the deciding factor (10), and are accepted the most easily. The educational influence of the team outlined here was described by Makarenko (7) as a method of parallel pedagogical influence and is the primary method in which the group influences the personality. "The parallelism of influence is the result of the fact that the demand of the educator is accepted by the group and both in this way have a parallel effect on each individual" (5:166). The group now becomes the co-educator; its members are engaged in a reciprocal education process. Individual players who develop with the help of the group also influence the team and contribute to its development. This is how the group is shaped and its members moulded. The ideology of the gorup is determined by mutually dependent factors, such as ideological atmosphere, public opinion, partner relationships, and the attitude of the team.

Often, when infactions against the norms and requirements of the team are committed, criticism and the ensuing demands are not dispensed. Errors made by individual members are often tolerated. One reason is that constructive criticism is not understood by everyone. Some athletes feel that it is "unfriendly" to criticize other players openly. These attitudes are occasionally still evident in inaccurate self-critical assessments,and in oversensitivity to criticism.

Let us briefly draw attention to some of the factors necessary to the creation of a constructively critical atmosphere.

1.   Coaches and trainers responsible for educating athletes must use constructive criticism and self-criticism in a way that sets an example to their players. Observations show that self-criticism, in particular, is not demonstrated properly. A coach who never admits to making a mistake cannot count on having a constructively critical atmosphere in the group he/she leads. Experience shows that mistakes which are admitted do not lead to a loss of authority, but instead

bring about an important improvement in the relationship between athlete and coach.

2. In order to develop a truly critical atmosphere, athletes must be encouraged to practise constructive criticism and self-criticism. For this reason, educators should regularly ask players for team and self-assessments to evaluate the strengths and weaknesses of all players.

3. A fundamental prerequisite for high level reciprocal education is an effective collective core team which functions as the "extended arm" of the educator. This brings a critical atmosphere into the group, which is necessary to influence the players. Coaches often have problems selecting this core team. The team should include members of the various social organizations. Team members should not be selected solely according to performance. Since education and influencing is primarily concerned with the development of personality traits, athletes with well-developed personality traits should be chosen. The strongest athletes, who normally enjoy the recognition so important for a team member, will not always display an enthusiastic willingness to perform or to complete the required activity. On the other hand, athletes who stand out because of exemplary enthusiasm may not always win the respect of teammates which is necessary to the reciprocal educational influencing. Forming this team is therefore an extremely complicated task which requires a maximum amount of pedagogical experience and an exact knowledge of the structure of the group which is to be led (3).

In conclusion, let us mention some of the various groups in the GDR to which athletes belong. Junior athletes are members of class or apprenticeship groups, Pioneers or the Free German Youth (FDJ), training groups, teams or possibly representative teams. Adult athletes are influenced by training groups, teams or representative teams, the FDJ, and student or workers groups. The decisive influence on the athletes' personalities are the training groups or teams (9). Their effectiveness, however, can be reduced by misconceptions, some of which may be shared by the entire team. Because of this, it is extremely important to ensure a uniform pedagogical procedure in the groups to which athletes belong.

All of the groups mentioned contribute to a positive attitude toward demands made in training and competition and parallelly influence political and ideological instruction. The knowledge and convictions which are so fundamental to education can be developed through unity in political and ideological sports objectives. Coaches and instructors, however, are by far the greatest influence in developing the massive potential of young athletes.

Coach's fair praise and criticism is very important in shaping athletes' behaviours. However, we observe that, even though praise has a highly stimulating effect on performance and behaviour of athletes, it is dispensed too seldom. On the other hand, criticism is used too often and, instead of solving conflicts, causes new ones.

Bibliography

Chapter 1

1. Döbler, H. Abriß einer Theorie der Sportspiele. DHfK. Leipzig 1969.
2. Kossakowski, A./Lompscher, J. Ideologisch-theoretische und methodologische Probleme der Pädagogischen Psychologie. Berlin 1971.
3. Pauli, R./Arnold, W. Pauli-Test, München 1951.

Chapter 2

1. Döbler, H. Die Bewegungsvorausnahme (Antizipation) beim Sportspiel. In: Theorie und Praxis der Körperkultur, 10 (1961) 11/12.
2. Galperin, P.J. Die Entwicklung der Untersuchungen über die Bildung geistiger Operationen. In: Ergebnisse der sowjetischen Psychologie, Akademie-Verlag, Berlin 1967.
3. Hacker, W. Allgemeine Arbeits- und Ingenieurpsychologie. VEB Deutscher Verlag der Wissenschaften, Berlin 1973.
4. Klaus, G. Kybernetik und Erkenntnistheorie. VEB Deutscher Verlag der Wissenschaften, Berlin 1972.
5. Klix, F. Information und Verhalten. VEB Deutscher Verlag der Wissenschaften, Berlin 1971.
6. Klix, F./u.a. Organismische Informationsverarbeitung. Akademie-Verlag, Berlin 1974.
7. Klix, F. Psychologische Beiträge zur Analyse kognitiver Prozesse. VEB Deutscher Verlag der Wissenschaften, Berlin 1976.
8. Konzag, G./u.a. Übungsformen für die Sportspiele. Sportverlag, Berlin 1979.
9. Konzag, I./Konzag G. Anforderungen an die kognitiven Funktionen in der psychischen Regulation sportlicher Spielhandlungen. In: Theorie und Praxis der Körperkultur, 29 (1980) 1.
10. Kossakowski, A./Ettrich, K.U. Psychologische Untersuchungen zur eigenständigen Handlungsregulation. VEB Deutscher Verlag der Wissenschaften, Berlin 1973.
11. Kossakowski, A./Lompscher, J. Teilfunktionen und Komponenten der psychischen Regulation der Tätigkeit. In: Autorenkollektiv: Psy-

chological Grundlagen der Persönlichkeitsentwicklung im pädagogischen Prozeß. Volk und Wissen VE Verlag, Berlin 1977.

12. Mahlo, F. Theoretische Probleme der taktischen Ausbildung in den Sportspielen. In: Theorie und Praxis der Körperkultur, 14 (1965) 9, 11, 12; 15 (1966) 1,2,3.
13. Puni, A.Z./Surkov, E.M. Theoretische Aspekte zur Antizipation in der Sportpsychologie. In: Theor. i. prakt. fiz. kult., Moskva 37 (1974) 7.
14. Purvanov, B. Einige Grundprobleme der Psychologie der Sportspiele (Übersicht). Medicina i fizkultura, Sofia 1966.
15. Rodionov, A.V. Der Sportler prognostiziert die Entscheidung. Fiskultura i sport, Moskau 1971.
16. Schmidt, H.-W. Leistungschance, Erfolgserwartung und Entscheidung. VEB Deutscher Verlag der Wissenschaften, Berlin 1966.
17. Trosanova, S. Untersuchungen der Antizipationsgenauigkeit bei der Bewegungstätigkeit von Volleyballern. In: Vupr. fiz. kult., Sofia 16 (1971) 6.

Chapter 3

1. Galperin, P.I. Zum, Problem der Aufmerksamkeit. In: Probleme der Ausbildung geistiger Handlungen. Volk und Wissen VE Verlag, Berlin 1972.
2. Kardos, L. Grundfragen der Psychologie und die Forschungen Pawlows. VEB Deutscher Verlag der Wissenschaften/Verlag der Ungarischen Akademie der Wissenschaften, Berlin/Budapest 1962.
3. Klix, F. Information und Verhalten. VEB Deutscher Verlag der Wissenschaften, Berlin 1971.
4. Konzag, G. Undersuchungen über die Aufmerksamkeitsverhältnisse im Basketball- und im Fußballspeil (Diss. A). M.-L.-U., Sektion Sportwissenschaft, Halle 1965.
5. Konzag, G. Aufmerksamkeit und Sport. Ein Beitrag zur theoretischen-Grundlegung der Sportpsychologie. (Diss. B). M.-L.-U., Sektion Sportwissenschaft, Halle 1974.
6. Kunath, P./Müller, G. Psychologische Aspekte der Betrachtung und Untersuchung des Handballsports. In: Med. u. Sport, XIV (1974) 2.
7. Maksimenko, C. Slatouster Experiment. In: Sportivnye igry, Moskva (1962) 3.
8. Olszewska, G. Über die Aufmerksamkeit von Spielern in den Sportspie-

larten In: Rocziniki Naukowe, Wysza Skola. Wychowynia Fizycznege
w Poznaniu. 19 (1971) 19.

9. Platonow, K.K. Psychologische Charakteristik des Sportlers. In: Theor. i.
    prakt. fiz. kult., Moskva 34 (1971) 1; (1971) 1.

10. Puni, A.Z. Abriß der Sportpsychologie. Sportverlag, Berlin 1961.

11. Puttrich, O./Friedrich, H. Anforderung und Beanspruchung bei industri-
    ellen Steuertätigkeiten unter analogieexperimentellen Bedingungen.
    In: Arb. psychol. u. wiss.-techn. Rev. Hrg.: Hacker/Skell/Straub,
    VEB Deutscher Verlag der Wissenschaften, Berlin 1968.

12. Reibetanz, K. Zur simultanen audiometrischen und pulsfrequenzanalytis-
    chen Bestinmmung der Belastungswirkungen geistiger Tätigkeiten.
    In: Autorenkollektiv: Psychologie in der sozialistischen Industrie.
    VEB Deutscher Verlag der Wissenschaften, Berlin 1971Game Situ-
    ation.

13. Reinhardt, W. Untersuchungen der Aufmerksamkeitsverhältnisse im
    Hallenhandballspiel. (Dipl. arb.) M.-L.-U., Sektion Sportswissen-
    schaft, Halle 1969.

14. Rodionow, A.W. Psychologie des sportlichen Zweikampfes. In: Fizkul'-
    tura i sport, Moskva 1968.

15. Rubinstein, S.L. Grundlagen der allgemeinen Psychologie. 8. Aufl., Volk
    u VE Verlag, Berlin 1973.

16. Rudik, P.A. Psychologie. Ein Lehrbuch fur Turnlehrer, Sportlehrer und
    Trainer. Volk und Wissen VE Verlag, Berlin 1963.

17. Schmidt, H.D. Empirische Forschungsmethoden der Pädagogik. Volk
    und Wissen VE Verlag, Berlin 1961.

18. Weingärtner, H. Untersuchungen der Aufmerksamkeitsverhältnisse im
    Volleyballspiel. (Dipl. arb.) M.-L.-U., Sektion Sportwissenschaft,
    Halle 1969.

Chapter 4

1. Angelow, W. Die Reaktionsschnelligkeit des Fußballspielers unter
    wettkampfnahen Bedingungen. In: Theorie und Praxis der Körper-
    erkultur, 11 (1962) 5,S. 447-456.

2. Clauß, G./u. a. Wörterbuch der Psychologie. VEB Bibliogr. Institut,
    Leipzig 1976.

3. Galperin, P.J. Die Entwicklung der Untersuchungen über die Bildung
    geistiger Operationen. In: Ergebnisse der sowjetischen Psychologie.

Akademie-Verlag, Berlin 1967.

4. Galperin, P.J. Die Psychologie des Denkens und die Lehre von der etappenweisen Ausbildung geistiger Prozesse. In: Untersuchungen des Denkens in der sowjetischen Psychologie. Volk und Wissen VE Verlag, Berlin 1967.

5. Geißler, H.-G./Klix, F. Psychologie Analysen geistiger Prozesse. VEB Deutscher Verlag der Wissenschaften, Berlin, 1974.

6. Gutjahr, W. Zur Messung psychischer Eigenschaften. VEB Deutscher Verlag der Wissenschaften, Berlin 1972.

7. Klix, F. Information und Verhalten. VEB Deutscher Verlag der Wissenschaften, Berlin 1971.

8. Klix, F./u.a. Organismische Informationsverarbeitung. Akademie-Verlag, Berlin 1974.

9. Klix, F. Psychologische Beiträge zur Analyse kognitiver Prozesse. VEB Deutscher Verlag der Wissenschaften, Berlin 1976.

10. Konzag, G. Aufmerksamkeit und Sport. In: Theorie und Praxis der Körperkultur, 24 (1975) 12, S. 1103-1112.

11. Konzag, I./Hennig, T. Die Anwendung von multivariaten Varianzanalysen und Diskriminanzanalysen bei der Lösung sportwissenschaftlicher Fragestellungen. Unv. Manuskript, Halle 1978.

12. Koşsakowski, A./Kühn, H./Lompscher, J./Rosenfeld, G. Psychologische Grundlagen der Persönlichkeitsentwicklung im pädagogischen Prozeß. Volk und Wissen VE Verlag, Berlin 1977.

13. Meili, R. Lehrbuch der psychologischen Diagnostik. H. Huber Verlag, Bern/Stuttgart 1965.

14. Purvanov, B. Einige Grundprobleme der Psychologie der Sportspiele. Medicina i fizkultura, Sofia 1966.

15. Rodionov, A.V. Psychodiagnostik sportlicher Fähigkeiten. Fiskultura i sport, Moskva, 1973.

16. Schmidt, H.-D. Leistungschance, Erfolgserwartung und Entscheidung. VEB Deutscher Verlag der Wissenschaften, Berlin 1966.

17. Witzlack, G. Grundlagen der Psychodiagnostik. VEB Deutscher Verlag der Wissenschaften, Berlin 1977.

Chapter 5

1. Esser, U./Förster, P. Über ein neues gruppenanalytisches Verfahren. Jugendforschung (1968) 6.

2. Friedrich, W. Methoden der marxistisch-leninistischen Sozialforschung. Berlin 1970.
3. Kunath, P./u.a. Beiträge zur Sportpsychologie, Bd. 2. Berlin 1974.
4. Lenk, H. Leistungsmotivation und Mannschaftsdynamik. Schorndorf 1970.
5. Lüschen (Hrsg.). Kleingruppenforschung und Gruppe im Sport. Köln 1966.
6. Münnich, I./Szakacz, F. Der Weg des Balles auf dem Feld. Budapest 1971.
7. Schellenberger, B. Die Bedeutung sozialer Beziehungen für das Verhalten und die Leistung der Sportler. In: Theorie und Praxis der Körperkultur, Berlin 20 (1971) 5.
8. Schellenberger, H. Das Gruppenbewertungsverfahren. In: Theorie und Praxis der Körperkultur, Berlin 22 (1973) 12.
9. Veit, H. Untersuchungen zur Gruppendynamik von Ballspeilmannschaften. Schorndorf 1971.
10. Vorwerg, M. Sozialpsychologische Strukturanalysen des Kollektivs. Berlin 1969.

Chapter 6

1. Bala, G.S. Der Einfluß von primären sozialen Einstellungen und Persönlichkeitsdimensionen auf Einstellungen gegenüber Sport. Schorndorf b. Stuttgart: Gymnasion 12 (1975) 4, S. 33-45.
2. Baum, L./Schellenberger, B. Einstellungen zu Sport und eigener sportlicher Betätigung. In: Theorie und Praxis der Körperkultur 18 (1969) 8, S. 706-718.
3. Fülle, S. Psychologische Probleme über die Einstellung zu den einzelnen Geräten bei Turnern. Leipzig: Dipl.-Arb. DHfK 1969.
4. Ilg, H. Das modifizierte Polaritätsprofil - eine Methode zur Erfassung sportlicher Einstellungen. In: Theorie und Praxis der Körperkultur 20 (1971) 11, S. 1007-1011.
5. Kirchgässner, H. Untersuchungen politisch-ideologischer und sportbezogener Einstellungen. In: Theorie und Praxis der Körperkultur 21 (1972) 8, S. 687-694.
6. Kossakowski, A./Lompscher, J. Ideologisch-theoretische und methodologische Probleme der Pädagogischen Psychologie. VEB Deutscher Verlag der Wissenschaften, Berlin 1973.

7. Matthesius, R. Methoden zur Erfassung aktuell erlebter Zustande - Das Polaritätsprofil. In: Beiträge zur Sportpsychologie, Bd. 1 Sportverlag, Berlin 1972, S. 112-121.

8. Medvedev, V.V./Rodionow, A.V./Chudadov, N.A. Psychologische Zustände während der sportlichen Tätigkeit. In: Theorie und Praxis der Körperkultur 23 (1974) 3, S. 234-248.

Chapter 7

1. Döbler, H. Abriß einer Theorie der Sportspiele. Anleitung für das Fernstudium. DHfK Leipzig 1969.

2. Hiebsch, H. und Vorwerg, M. Einführung in die marxistische Sozialpsychologie. 2. Auflage, VEB Deutscher Verlag der Wissenschaften, Berlin 1967.

Chapter 8

1. Thieß, G./Schnabel, G./Baumann, R. Training von A bis Z. Kleines Wörterbuch für die Theorie und Praxis des sportlichen Trainings. 2. Auflage. Sportverlag, Berlin 1980.

2. Kollektiv. Wörterbuch der Psychologie. 1. Auflage. Leipzig 1976.

Chapter 9

1. Bachman, W. Zur Psychologie des Kollektivs. In: Deutsche Zeitschrift für Philosophie. 12 (1964) 5, S. 559.

2. Boshowitsch, I.L. Die Persönlichkeit und ihre Entwicklung im Schulater. Berlin 1970, S. 93.

3. Hiebsch, H./Vorwerg, M. Einführung in die marxistische Sozialpsychologie. Berlin 1966.

4. Hofstätter, P.R. Gruppendynamik. Rowohlt, Hamburg 1961.

5. Karpinski, G. Die Gruppenentropie - ein Maß für den Anteil unterschiedlicher Aufgabenbereiche an der Strukturierung von Spielsportkollektiven. In: Theorie und Praxis der Körperkultur 24 (1975) 8.

6. Kossakowski, A./Otto, K. Psychologie Untersuchungen zur Entwicklung sozialistischer Persönlichkeiten. Berlin 1971.

7. Krause, B./Lander, H.-J. Zur Faktoranalyse. In: Probl. u. Ergebn. der

Psychologie (1971) 31.

8. Kunath, P. Sozialpsychologische Komponenten der sportlichen Leistung. In: Beiträge zur Sportpsychologie 2. Sportverlag, Berlin 1974., S. 19.
9. Rubinstein, S.L. Sein und Bewußtsein. Akademie-Verlag, Berlin 1962, S. 206.

Chapter 10

1. Frester, R. Grundgedanken der Entwicklung des klassischen autogenen Trainings und seine Anwendung im Sport. In: Beiträge zur Sportpsychologie, Bd. 1. Sportverlag, Berlin 1972.
2. Frester, R. Ideomotorisches Training im Sport. In: Beiträge zur Sportpsychologie, Bd. 2. Sportverlag, Berlin 1974.
3. Schellenberger, H. Psychoregulative Verfahren im Sport. In: Studienmaterial Sportpshychologie - Fachausbildung. DHfK Leipzig 1978.

Chapter 11

1. Döbler, H. Abriß einer Theorie der Sportspiele. Leipzig 1963.
2. Guthke, J. Zur Diagnostik der intellektuellen Lernfähigkeit. Berlin 1977.
3. Hacker, W. Allgemeine Arbeits- und Ingenieurpsychologie. Berlin 1978.
4. Horn, E. Spelling. Encycl. Educ. Res. New York 1941, S. 1116-1183.
5. Kossakowski, A./Otto, K.-H. Psychologische Untersuchungen zur Entwicklung sozialistischer Persönlichkeit. Berlin 1978.
6. Lenin, W.I. Werke, Bd. 26. Berlin 1961.
7. Mahlo, F. Theoretische Probleme der taktischen Ausbildung in den Sportspielen. In: Theorie und Praxis der Körperkultur 14 (1965) 11, S. 970-979.
8. Mahlo, F. Die Ausbildung von Spielfahigkeiten im Sportunterricht. Körpererziehung, Berlin (1974) 12, S, 550-558.
9. Pauli, R./Arnold, W. Pauli-Test, München 1951.
10. Peglau, S. Testanleitung - Tachistokopischer Wahrnehmungstest (unv. Manuskript).
11. Raven, J.C. Guide to using the coloured progressiv metrices. London 1948.
12. Thieß, G./Schnabel, G./Baumann, R. Training von A bis Z. Kleines Wörterbuch für die Theorie und Praxis des sportlichen Trainings. 2.

Auflage. Sportverlag, Berlin 1980.

Chapter 12

1. Budzisch, M. Erzieherisch wirksame Kenntnisvermittlung und -aneignung im Sportunterricht und im außerunterrichtlichen Sport. In: Sozialistische Erziehung im Schulsport. Volk und Wissen VE Verlag, Berlin 1976.

2. Döbler, H. Beiträge zur Theorie und Methodik der Sportspeile unter besonderer Berücksichtigung des Fußballtrainings. DHfK Leipzig, 1975, S. 30.

3. Förster, P. Gruppendiagnostik. In: Der sozialwissenschaftliche Forschungsprozeß. Herausgegeben von Friedrich, W./Hennig, W. VEB Deutscher Verlag der Wissenschaften, Berlin 1975, S. 562 ff.

4. Hiebsch, H./Vorwerg, M. Einführung in die marxistische Sozialpsychologie. VEB Deutscher Verlag der Wissenschaften, Berlin 1971, S. 126 ff.

5. Klimpel, P. Erziehung und Entwicklung der Persönlichkeit. Volk und Wissen VE Verlag, Berlin 1969, S. 166.

12. Schwidtmann, H./Kogel. Die Vorbildwirkung des Lehrers - eine wesent-liche Bedingung für die Erziehung der Schüler zu sozialistischen Persönlichkeiten. In: Körpererziehung 23 (1973), S. 568-573.

13. Scurkova, N.E. Gespräche über Erziehung (I). In: Theorie und Praxis der Körperkultur. 23 (1974) 10, S. 918-919.

14. Scurkova, N.E. Gespräche über Erziehung (II). In: Theorie und Praxis de Körperkultur. 23 (1974) 11, S. 986.

15. Stolz/Herrmann/Müller. Beiträge zur Theorie der sozialistischen Erziehung. Volk und Wissen VE Verlag,Berlin 1971, S. 295.

16. Thieß, G./Schnabel, G./Baumann, R. Training von A bis Z. Kleines Wörterbuch für die Theorie und Praxis des sportlichen Trainings. 2. Auflage. Sportverlag, Berlin 1980.